Flannery O'Connor's Dark Comedies

Southern Literary Studies
Louis D. Rubin, Jr., Editor

CAROL SHLOSS

Flannery O'Connor's Dark Comedies

The Limits of Inference

Louisiana State University Press
BATON ROUGE AND LONDON

Designer: Joanna Hill
Typeface: VIP Garamond Book
Typesetter: G & S Typesetters, Inc.
Printer: Thomson-Shore, Inc.
Binder: John H. Dekker & Sons

Grateful acknowledgment is made for permission to quote from
S. Kathleen Feeley, *Flannery O'Connor: Voice of the Peacock* (New
Brunswick: Rutgers University Press, 1972) and Miles Orvell, *Invisible Parade: The Fiction of Flannery O'Connor* (Philadelphia: Temple University Press, 1972). Selections from *Everything That Rises
Must Converge* by Flannery O'Connor. Copyright © 1956, 1957,
1958, 1960, 1961, 1962, 1964, 1965 by the Estate of Mary Flan-
nery O'Connor. Selections from *The Habit of Being: The Letters of
Flannery O'Connor*, selected and edited by Sally Fitzgerald. Copyright © 1979 by Regina O'Connor. Selections from *Mystery and
Manners* by Flannery O'Connor. Copyright © 1957, 1961, 1963,
1964, 1966, 1967, 1969 by the Estate of Mary Flannery O'Connor.
Copyright © 1962 by Flannery O'Connor. Copyright © 1961 by
Farrar, Straus and Cudahy, Inc. (now Farrar, Straus and Giroux,
Inc.). Selections from *The Violent Bear It Away* by Flannery
O'Connor. Copyright © 1955, 1960 by Flannery O'Connor. Selec-
tions from *Wise Blood* by Flannery O'Connor. Copyright © 1952,
1962 by Flannery O'Connor. Reprinted by permission of Farrar,
Straus and Giroux, Inc., and the Harold Matson Company, Inc.

LIBRARY OF CONGRESS CATALOGING IN PUBLICATION DATA

Shloss, Carol.
    Flannery O'Connor's dark comedies.

    (Southern literary studies)
    Bibliography: p.
    Includes index.
    1. O'Connor, Flannery—Criticism and interpretation.
I. Title.   II. Series.
PS3565.C57Z86   813'.54   80-10609
ISBN 0-8071-0674-7

To the memory of Philip Rahv

Contents

Acknowledgments

I would like to thank Aileen Ward and Robert Fitzgerald for their encouragement during the early stages of this book. I am also grateful to Richard Ohmann, Alfred Turco, and Geraldine Murphy for their comments and interest, to Wesleyan University for assistance in preparing the manuscript, and to my editors at Louisiana State University Press. And I owe special thanks to Jan Schreiber for his thorough and patient concern throughout.

Flannery O'Connor's Dark Comedies

"What is language at all but a convention?" said Isabel.
"She has the good taste not to pretend, like some peo-
ple I have met, to express herself by original signs."
Henry James
The Portrait of a Lady

The literary critic, like the historian, is compelled to
treat every religion in the same way that religions treat
each other, as though it were a human hypothesis,
whatever else he may in other contexts believe it to be.
Northrop Frye
Anatomy of Criticism

Introduction

Several years ago a Dutch naturalist and a friend set out to photograph the tracks left on the sand of dunes by various creatures and to reconstruct the stories they reveal. One photograph in their book shows the footprints of a bird on wind-rippled sand. At first the marks are light and evenly spaced; suddenly they become erratic and pronounced, turn at a sharp angle, and disappear. Presumably the bird was walking peacefully until alarmed; the walk then turned to a hop, and finally the bird took off on its wings. Even the amateur observer can read this skeletal story from the sand, but we are told that the naturalists could significantly extend this detective work. The particular shape of the prints allowed them to identify the bird as an oyster catcher. Further, they knew that a bird cannot take off except precisely against the wind. At the time of the event, therefore, the wind must have blown from the direction to which the tracks turn. But there is an apparent incongruity in the photograph, for the ripples in the sand were formed by a wind coming from the bird's initial direction of walking. Accordingly, the authors made another conjecture: there was a change of wind between the times in which the ripples and the footprints were formed.[1]

This anecdote is recounted to illustrate the extent to which perception is an actively constructive rather than a passive process, for the interpretation of the original configuration in the sand varied according to the prior knowledge of the apprehenders. To the uninformed observer, the tracks told of an animal in flight; to the trained analyst, the same prints offered a more extended comment on species and environmental conditions.

Unlike the traces of nature, the artist's trace is made with the intention of being interpretable. In literature it is deliberately executed and delivered by means of linguistic conventions to facilitate the process of reconstruction. But there is this analogy between the tracks on the beach and a work of art: any picture—whether a visual or a verbal canvas—contains a good deal less information than the object it represents would exhibit.[2] It is by virtue of prior knowledge that we construe the conventions of representation in fuller measure than is literally warranted, and we do this all the time, and usually without thinking. When, for example, Henry James describes Lord Warburton in *The Portrait of a Lady* as having "a noticeably handsome face, fresh-coloured, fair, and frank, with firm, straight features, a lively grey eye and the rich adornment of a chestnut beard," he has not expressed all the details of Warburton's physique; but we infer, nonetheless, that he is a normal human being with all parts intact, capable of behaving in customary ways. This process of filling in, of adding to what is literally unstated in the text, is accomplished by means of inference. Simply defined, inference is that principle by which we can reasonably expect that one condition will follow on the occurrence of another—the trees are wet: it has been raining; there are ashes in the fireplace: a log has been burned.[3] Without going into the subtleties of this process, I would like to reconsider the initial example of constructive intelligence in relation to the natural world. For in the natural situation, it was clearly established that there is a pointed relationship between the conclusions of inference and the mental resources of the perceiver. So it is with art. The mind of the apprehender has a marked effect on the encounter with what is given—the artist's trace.

Granted this correlation, it becomes of central importance for a writer to identify his audience; those who will interpret his fictional signs will do so by decoding the given skeleton of words in complex combination with preexistent assumptions. An author must consider not only what can be inferred from a text but what will be deduced from it, given a certain model reader.

In the case of Flannery O'Connor, there is ample record of the artist's perception of her position vis-à-vis an imagined reader. This information is particularly significant, because she wrote from a minority stance, as an ardent believer who lived in a predominantly nontheistic society. We know, for example, that she wrote primarily for those whose point of view varied from her own religious one, and as she considered, varied because of a radical ignorance. "My audience are the people who think God is dead," she wrote to a friend in 1955; "at least these are the people I am conscious of writing for."[4] Her intentional traces were left, not for the trained naturalist, but for the casual walker on the beach, with the obvious distinction that we are no longer discussing biological tracks and untrained naturalists, but intentionally devised language and readers without a religious bias. But in either case, the same principle obtains: we cannot reconstruct where we do not know what is possible. In the same way that we cannot infer wind direction from the oyster catcher's footprints unless we know a generalization about bird flight, we cannot infer anagogical meaning in a text unless we are accustomed to reading such signs in fiction and have the information to do so.

In response to the distance between the beliefs of author and reader, several critics have concluded that the encounter of theologically uninformed readers with O'Connor's texts is "not only partial but wrong."[5] They insist on a reader whose perceptions are already in harmony with the author's or who will educate himself in order to read correctly. There is no doubt, in the case of the oyster catcher, that the trained naturalist was able to infer the fuller picture from the evidence of the bird's tracks. And it is tempting to say that a similar kind of extended and specialized knowledge would contribute to a richer understanding of O'Connor's work, but for one fact that must be returned to with a full understanding of its implications: Flannery O'Connor did not use the Christian as her model reader. As she observed, "We must remember that [the novelist's] vision has to be transmitted and that the limitations and blind spots of his audience will very definitely affect the way he is able to show what he sees." Since she addressed herself precisely to those who were untutored in religious belief, it is in terms of those readers that one must evaluate the success of her rhetoric, the viability of the artistic "traces" created to ensure a certain reconstruction of the artist's reality.[6]

In this kind of inquiry, the facts of the artist's life are less relevant than the state of her belief, but O'Connor's personal position is interesting in itself and germane to speculations about her motivations as a writer. She was born in Savannah, Georgia, in 1925, the only daughter of Edward and Regina Cline O'Connor. Her education until graduate school at the Iowa Writers' Workshop was parochial. Since she was the child of an ardent Catholic family, this is perhaps not surprising. St. Vincent's School in Savannah was succeeded by the Sacred Heart School in Milledgeville, where the family moved in the late thirties. Later she went to the local Georgia Women's College.

Her determination to write may have come in early childhood, but it is impossible to know more than that she was an energetic participant in college literary activities, both as editor and contributor, offering cartoons and commentary with the sardonic humor that we now recognize as characteristic.[7] From Iowa she went to Yaddo, and from there to New York City. The move to New York was the rather predictable action of a young girl undertaking a literary career. What is surprising is the brevity of the stay, the decision to exchange whatever advantages the city might have offered in the way of friendship, encouragement, and professional contacts for the celibate existence of a country boarder. Robert and Sally Fitzgerald reminisce fondly about the year she spent on their Connecticut farm, living spartanly in the room over their garage. The time is recalled as a happy one for them, full of pleasant country routines, babies, reading, and long, lighthearted discussions in the evening. They included Flannery in these activities graciously and naturally, but it is significant that she remarked of the situation that the children probably perceived the adults as "he," "she," and "the other one." [8]

In some senses, she always remained "the other one," for the circumstances of her health dictated a life of sustained isolation. In 1950 on the train to Georgia for Christmas vacation, she became terribly sick. She had, as it turned out, disseminated lupus, the blood disease that had killed her father years earlier.

From this point, the contours of O'Connor's life were established in an austere pattern. Though the disease was held in abeyance, this was accomplished by means of extensive medication and a restricted daily regimen. A strong and resolute woman, Regina O'Connor moved herself and her ailing daughter to the family farm where, with brief visits to friends and universities and one trip to Lourdes, Flannery remained until her death in 1964.

Regina O'Connor still lives in Milledgeville and has received a good number of O'Connor disciples who came, in all good faith, "in search of Flannery O'Connor." Of the daily routine there is little doubt: Flannery wrote in the mornings and drove to town at noon to lunch with her mother at the Sanford House; afternoons she spent outdoors, caring for the numerous chickens and peafowl that became her idiosyncratic passion. But the search has always been for something more, for signs of the woman's character, for clues toward attitudes and the acceptance of what was surely an ill-favored fate—to live through thirteen years with the uninterrupted consciousness of imminent demise. Here, facing the question of personality, admirers have usually felt uncertain, forced to rely on anecdote and brief glimpses for indications of the deeper life.[9] Inevitably they have resorted to the accounts of relatives and occasional friends who have their own biases and reasons for preserving a certain image of the writer in their midst.

Was O'Connor, as her mother would have us understand, the perfect lady, well mannered and reserved, respectful of family custom, always self-contained, good humored, and witty?[10] Was she the self-effacing soul who would rather prattle cheerfully in correspondence than admit any pain?[11] How deep was the anger that Josephine Hendin sees in her scowling, reluctant participation in the sociability expected of genteel southern women?[12] Clearly she was "the other one" by inclination, illness, and profession; but did she experience this role in the satisfactory sense that Regina O'Connor praises (her mother claims that she always waited until her friends came to her), or was she simply unable to face and discuss her loneliness? On this level, biography must be purely speculative. We know for certain that she was sustained by a deep religious faith and that she did not voice public complaints about the circumstances that forced all her adult years into the pattern of extended childhood. In fact, she once snapped out, "The disease is of no consequence to my writing, since for that I use my head and not my feet."[13] On another occasion, she remarked: "Most writers have had many obstacles put in their way. I have had none. . . . There has been no interesting or noble struggle. The only thing I wrestle with is the language and a certain poverty of means in handling it, but this is merely what you have to do to write at all."[14] But these are almost evasive answers, concentrating on the physical circumstances of composition rather than the emotional and intellectual preconditions of writing. In another sense, it is clear that incurable illness did shape her sensibilities, providing her, if only by limitation, with the themes and obsessive concerns of the fiction—the mother-child relationship, the position of the widowed farm woman, the intricacies of social hierarchy in the racially sensitive South. Of equal interest, however, is the sensibility that must have been fostered by prolonged physical vulnerability, those conditions which must have led to the remark that "death has always been brother to my imagination." [15] Her conclusion in "A Memoir of Mary Ann" is certainly as aptly applied to her own situation as to that of the brave, cancer-ridden child, that the nuns had completed the only training of relevance to the girl: "an education for death." [16]

Flannery O'Connor died in the Piedmont Hospital in Atlanta, Georgia, on August 3, 1964. With the exception of the six stories that constituted her master's thesis at Iowa and early portions of her first novel, *Wise Blood*, all her published work was written in Georgia between the onset of her illness and her death. In the title story of O'Connor's first collection of fiction, *A Good Man Is Hard to Find*, the Misfit remarks of an old grandmother he has just killed, "She would of been a good woman . . . if it had been somebody there to shoot her every minute of her life." [17] The implication is clearly that consciousness of mortality is the essential prerequisite for virtue. It is tempting to extend the fiction into a statement relevant to the life of its author, for the impetus and mode of perception manifest in most of O'Connor's deeply engaging but violent stories do not seem to arise from either social anger or love. They seem to come rather from the need to wean oneself from social particulars through harsh comedy and to face "every minute" the ultimate ravishment of the flesh.

As interesting as these biographical speculations may be, it is not Flannery O'Connor's life that concerns us here, or the themes of the stories, or even the elusive transformations of experience into fiction, but the narrative methods of embodying a point of view. Biography can furnish tentative motives for the broad outlines of fiction—O'Connor's preoccupation with death or with southern women in certain predicaments—but it cannot account for procedures, for the particular modes of expression that a writer adopts in consequence of his perceptions. Given the theological relativity that characterizes the contemporary social milieu, any writer of religious sensibility is inevitably forced into the role of rhetorician. If one of the aims of writing is to communicate the spiritual, then the concern of writers must be to find ways of rendering that not only allow the text to be read on an anagogical level, but make such a reading inevitable.

My concern, then, is to locate and discuss O'Connor's methods of embodying spiritual meanings and, conversely, to articulate the ways in which readers encounter these rhetorical devices and use them as a basis for inferring secondary levels of implication in a text. The emphasis is to be placed, not on the individual reader's idiosyncratic associations, but on the qualities inherent in the work of art that are capable of eliciting certain reading responses.[18] Since biography and the writer's creative development are of less importance than identifying the mechanisms of aesthetic response, the procedure is neither chronological nor inclusive. In the thirty-one stories and two novels O'Connor wrote in her lifetime, certain major rhetorical techniques may be identified—hyperbole, distortion, allusion, analogy, the dramatization of extreme religious experience, the manipulation of judgment through narrative voice, and direct address to the reader. These fictional techniques are to be found in most of O'Connor's writings, but only the stories that bring these qualities into sharp relief are discussed.[19]

Chapters One and Two establish a context for discussing the fiction by indicating what O'Connor wanted to achieve through her art, her perception of her audience, and the problems inherent in her aims. In these chapters, the commentary is essentially theoretical, and it is applicable to a wider range of fictional situations than the one at hand. For this reason, it does not include many examples from O'Connor's own writing, which come in the later chapters that deal with specific stories and novels. The conclusions follow from exploring the implications of the remark often made so casually about these stories—that nothing in them compels a theological reading.[20]

ONE

The Problem of Textual Implication

I

Robert Fitzgerald closed his memoir of his young friend Flannery O'Connor with the comment: "I do not want to claim too much for these stories [*Everything That Rises Must Converge*] or to imply that every story comes off equally well. That would be unfaithful to her own sense of conscience and sense of fact."[1] Considering the private and professional ties that must have held them, it is a cautious, self-restrained remark. Fitzgerald wanted to represent accurately the achievement of an artist for whom accurate representation was an essential ingredient of craftsmanship. In so doing, he may well have understated enthusiasm in the interests of truth. As he saw it, his respect was manifested not in unqualified praise but in seeing clearly, without the prejudices of friendship, the contours and merits of her prose.

Fitzgerald's moderation is notable, for it is a sensibility not always shared by other critics of O'Connor. Admirers of her work or adherents of her religion, they have often read the signs of their own faith into the prose, underestimating the nature of the problem that O'Connor faced with a direct and hesitant candor—that of the religious writer in a culture untutored in religious ritual and symbolism and uncomfortable with the inexplicable aspects of human experience.

By admitting the orthodoxy of her religious perspective, O'Connor may have unwittingly invited the kinds of criticism she received.[2] Wilfrid Sheed remarked:

> I question the wisdom of writers coming all the way out of the closet—any closet. Having been recently accused of closet Christianity myself, I speak with feeling about closets. Graham Greene and Evelyn Waugh stuck their heads briefly out of the Christian one and had to fight their way back in. Because, in an instant, the scavengers had their number—they were *Catholic* novelists, which explained everything: every plot twist, every two-bit *apercu*. The uncreative are grateful for these skeleton keys. Originality is promptly flattened like tinfoil. Catholic novelist, Catholic *woman* novelist: the more words you can pile up front, the less remains to be done.[3]

The writer who announces his personal circumstances exposes himself to the possibility that this information will be used critically to explain the procedures of his fiction. Not all of O'Connor's previous critics have been uncreative scavengers for the biographical key to interpretation, but a number of them have not adequately discriminated among the writing conventions that can either facilitate or hinder the embodiment of metaphysical concerns.

Just as there is a history of mimesis in literature—a progression in the techniques for representing reality—so there has been a development in the conventions of writing that enable an author to present spiritual significance.[4] Because the religious writer no longer communicates with most of his readers on the basis of shared assumptions about the mystical extensions of reality, but rather in spite of cognitive differences, the study of anagogical fiction must now inevitably include an evaluation of rhetorical effect. Joseph Conrad, whom O'Connor took as a literary model, comments in his famous preface to *The Nigger of the Narcissus*: "My task which I am trying to achieve is, by the power of the written word, to make you hear, to make you feel—it is, before all, to make you *see*. That—and no more and it is everything."[5] The procedures of changing vision, of altering a reader's perspective through a literary experience, must be developed within a context: for the contemporary reading audience, reality is coextensive with the visible; for the spiritual writer, the natural world is important primarily as it suggests an invisible order. O'Connor was well aware of this, and the discrepancy between her own extended sense of reality and a secular point of view was what concerned her.

> The setting in which most modern fiction takes place is
> exactly a setting in which nothing is so little felt to be
> true as the reality of a faith in Christ. . . . Fiction may
> deal with faith implicitly but explicitly it deals only
> with faith-in-a-person, or persons. What must be un-
> questionable is what is implicitly implied as the au-
> thor's attitude, and to do this the writer has to succeed
> in making the divinity of Christ seem consistent with
> the structure of all reality. This has to be got across
> implicitly in spite of a world that doesn't feel it, in spite
> of characters who don't live it.[6]

This situation makes the literary forms of heightened emphasis a necessary concern for a Christian artist. He must prove in his writing what, at another more religious time, he might have counted on his readers to understand.

O'Connor was concerned with providing a believable imitation of life. She strove to give accurate reference and adequate motivation to characters and events, but she also admitted that, for the serious fiction writer, "the meaning of [the] story does not begin except where these things have been exhausted."[7] Her aim, stated simply, was to raise a structure of anagogical meaning over the literal action of the stories, to construct natural tales that were sacred in implication.

II

But the procedures for achieving such intentions are not clear-cut. The secular context of O'Connor's writing immediately poses two interpretive problems that must be anticipated by a religious artist who wants to write effectively: one of plausibility and one of cognition.

Northrop Frye gives the general name *displacement* to the devices used by the mythic artist to meet demands for literary credibility. His explanation of this concept is based on the assumption that mythic modes continue to exist in our culture, but in altered forms: "The central principle of displacement is that what can be metaphorically identified in a myth can only be linked in [contemporary fiction] by some form of simile: analogy, significant association, incidental accompanying imagery and the like. In a myth, we can have a sun-god or a tree-god; in a romance we may have a person who is significantly associated with the sun or trees. In more realistic modes, the association becomes less significant and more a matter of incidental, even coincidental imagery."[8] In other words, as literary works increase in realistic representation, the accessibility of mythic patterns decreases. Thus a literary work that is both plausible and unambiguously mythic is logically impossible since the very use of realistic technique signals the displacement of the myth, which deals with something outside the everyday, realistic world. To illustrate his point, Frye cites a reading of *The Marble Faun* that overlooks this inverse relationship. Hawthorne's central character, Hilda, is gentle; doves are fond of her; another character calls her his dove. Yet the critic who concludes that Hilda is a dove-goddess like Venus errs by translating literature from one mode to another, by reading romance as straight myth. To the contrary, Frye would have us understand that the structure of fiction contains inherent conceptual implications. If it is written in terms closely associated with human experience, it is to be read in terms of human rather than divine actions. A literary mode that submerges or disguises myth in the interests of plausibility does so with the observable effect that emphasis rests on realistic context and representation.

While this discussion of the relation between realism and myth is cursory, it is clear that, given an intention to make the surface actions of fiction credible, the techniques available to O'Connor for portrayal of Christian myth were ones of indirection. There are more ways to suggest the divine than the use of similes, but Frye's central observation is still credible: myth, which deals with the miraculous, and realism, which deals with the probable, are extremes of a progression of literary form, and fiction that seeks to encompass them both will inevitably achieve an uneasy focus.

The problem is not merely one of theory. This janus-faced intention can create perceptual obstacles for a reader. The more realistic the text, the more realism will serve as a sufficient basis for interpretation. To see why, it is only necessary to ask what aspects of a basically realistic text signal that a secondary, mythic meaning is submerged and relevant to the correct understanding of the work. Heraclitus wrote, "The Lord whose oracle is at Delphi neither speaks nor conceals, but gives signs." [9] It is the tradition in anagogical readings of biblical texts to interpret such signs, to attribute spiritual meanings to literal events. [10] But there is an essential distinction between such efforts and the reading of prose fiction, for the religious scholar assumes a priori that events and images do symbolize or point to a correlative spiritual significance. The endeavor is then to discover which assignment of meaning is most appropriate, given that presupposition. On the other hand, in reading fiction, no one agrees or should be asked to agree in advance to look for anything more than the text suggests in itself.

Bearing this distinction in mind, it would seem that unless one began as a believer, spiritual implications in prose fiction, however consciously intended by an author, might well remain uncued and therefore undiscovered. In fact, there is evidence that this often happened in the early days of O'Connor criticism; for the publication of her first Christian essay, "The Fiction Writer and His Country," dramatically changed the tenor of critical response. Until that time in 1957, spiritual meanings usually went unheeded in her texts, and commentary consisted of reserved appreciations of her skill in "drawing unusual portraits of unusual characters." [11] O'Connor's letters in those early years are filled with anxious jokes about the critical reception of her work. "I seem to attract the lunatic fringe," she wrote to Sally and Robert Fitzgerald; and to another friend she admitted, "I am mighty tired of reading reviews that call *A Good Man* brutal and sarcastic." Repeatedly she noted cases of what she considered misreadings. "I just read another review from a Kansas City paper that ended with the sentence: 'These stories are technically excellent; spiritually empty.'" [12]

She was obviously dismayed, though John Hawkes and Nathan Scott, Jr., among very few, suggested that the young Georgian's principal concern might be anagogical; but Hawkes's review followed months of personal correspondence. In 1971, when Leon Driskell and Joan Brittain observed that "Miss O'Connor's protestation of Christian orthodoxy at least provided a starting place for the critics to get at her work," they implicitly admitted that the fiction did not seem to support a spiritual reading in and of itself. [13] But they were right: that essay and others like it did give critics a handle, and since then criticism often has taken statements of faith in her essays as the key to correlative spiritual meanings in her fiction. Working in the manner of biblical exegetes, armed with this privileged and extraneous knowledge, such critics rarely display doubt that submerged meanings of a certain type exist. These few examples illustrate that trend:

> If Miss O'Connor's fiction is successfully anagogical, as her critical comments show she intended it to be, then some form of anagogical reading of it would be necessary. The reader who responded to a single level of meaning would be responding not only partially, but wrongly; he would be denying her central assumptions about existence. [14]

> Any attempt at an appreciation of her work must begin with a clear understanding of this Christian theme; regardless of one's own religious predilections, he must know the meaning of the sacramental view of life before he can know the meaning of Flannery O'Connor's fiction. [15]

> Because her work is . . . wholly "of the Christian," it has
> what Flannery herself called "an added dimension," . . .
> an anagogical level of meaning.[16]

But assuming that the inevitable achievement of a Christian artist is
a religious literature is, as W. K. Wimsatt has shown, an "intentional
fallacy," and such criticism also misrepresents O'Connor's own
position that "the intentions of the writer have to be found in the
work itself and not in his life."[17] At another time she remarked to a
close friend, "Yes'm she don't get the moral point. But the reason
she don't is because I have failed to make it plain. . . . You understand Thomas [in "The Comforts of Home"] because you know me;
she doesn't understand Thomas because she just has the story to
read and understand."[18] To require that a reader share the artist's
beliefs or that he construe the meaning of a story from extrinsic
commentary is to insist on bypassing the fiction as a linguistic construct with inherent meanings.

Is the biographical information gleaned from these essays the
most effective starting point of criticism? It seems better to remember that language is communal, effective to the extent that writer
and reader construe it similarly. Consequently, a writer's "sacramental view" is immaterial unless it can be embodied in, that is,
translated into, writing techniques that permit its discovery by
readers. The central issue seems really to be a matter of determining what kinds of evidence intrinsic to the text can indicate that
several levels of meaning are operative.[19] For this reason, it is useful
to consider anagogy as a special category of implication, that is, as
one of a variety of possible secondary meanings that may be inferred from a text. Looked at in this way, spiritual implication
should be discoverable from procedures that guide any transformation, by inference, from the primary or literal level of writing to a
level of further significance. When secondary meanings are seen as
derivations, or as extensions, of conventional meaning identifiable
from particular conditions in the literal sense of the prose, no intui-
tive "leaps" or privileged knowledge of intent should be required
for their interpretation. Instead, the necessary connection between

the literal event and its anagogical significance should be signaled by the text itself. When the problem is posed in this manner, the reader is no longer faced with the need to concur a priori with O'Connor's beliefs, nor does he need to know whether the author had a certain attitude in life. The question is simply whether the prose "can be construed as having a particular social meaning," a meaning that may include a metaphysical dimension but one that is nonetheless accessible to all, regardless of religious inclination.[20]

III

As a way of identifying the semantic clues capable of directing interpretation away from the literal events of a text to something more abstract, more general, or more metaphysical, consider a brief description in T. S. Eliot's *The Waste Land*.

> You know only
> A heap of broken images, where the sun beats
> And the dead tree gives no shelter, the cricket no
>   relief,
> And the dry stone no sound of water.[21]

We know from common usage that the word *stone* in line 5 signifies a solid mass of earthy matter. Although the word has a number of other meanings—a jewel, or a hard, natural growth in an animal—the context of natural description indicates that the first definition is the most appropriate. This does not imply that having made this initial identification, the reader must conjure up an image of the particular rock that Eliot was thinking of. The poet probably did not have any one object in mind when he wrote the lines. He did, however, write with the assurance that the word indicated a type, that it was an entity with a boundary of meaning, a set of implications—hardness, range of size, weight—by which one could classify or exclude something as a stone. In other words, he intended to communicate via a learned convention of language.[22] But what is the further significance of the word? As it appears in the poem, does the stone have any special implications beyond those characteristics identifiable by common usage? Could we tell, for example, if it has any "sacred" qualities? In this regard, there are several relevant observations about its use. Eliot's stone is a dry stone—he uses an adjective to describe it—and it appears as part of a list that delineates the boundaries of the addressed person's awareness. "You know only" broken images, dead trees, dry stones. Furthermore, these things are implicitly contrasted to an opposite setting of quietness, shelter, and moisture. Despite this patterning, it is impossible to infer anything more than what is literally stated, and were the lines to be encountered out of the larger context of the poem, one would be forced to conclude that they discuss the knowledge of a desert dweller. Only by reading more of the poem does one come to identify these images of barren landscape with the emotional or spiritual poverty of a civilization. Given that clue, *dry stone* signifies some part of cultural deprivation. The characteristic of stone—that it cannot sustain life—is identified as the one aspect of "stoneness" most related to the theme of social aridity. Notice, however, that the implication or secondary meaning is intrinsic to the word *stone*. The context does not create a special, new meaning for the word; rather it indicates what, among the many qualities of "stoneness," is to be emphasized or brought into focus. By the same token, the context acts as a sieve or strainer, establishing the grounds that exclude irrelevant considerations such as the rock's size or shape. By the methods of direct modification, juxtaposition, and contrast, then, Eliot has refined the meaning of the word and directed our understanding of it.

The purpose of this brief critical exercise is to interpret implication in a case where the submerged meaning in the word sequence is contained in the language of the poem's initial formulation. Generally, the impetus to emphasize a particular characteristic of stone (and for that matter, dead trees and sun-parched land) comes from the perception of incongruity. The juxtaposition of events in the poem, taken literally, is illogical. Why speak about a desert in the midst of sundry events in London? Consequently a reader proceeds to discover points of possible similarity between objects and events, between location and location, which will make a unified statement (albeit one that unifies by selective exclusion) possible. In other literary circumstances, perception of improbability or incompleteness on the literal level of events might prompt additional inquiry of this sort.[23]

Remaining for the time being on the level of theory, what relevance do these observations have for deciphering Flannery O'Connor's writing? For it is likely that inconsistency, improbability, or incompleteness on the literal level of exposition would alert a reader of her fiction to intended extensions of meaning. The difficulty arises from the direction of interpretation O'Connor required of her readers. From what we know of her aims in fiction writing, she did intend to use language in the manner suggested by Eliade, to effect a "transformation of an object into a sign of mystery."[24] While the procedures of understanding that were scrutinized with T. S. Eliot's poetry worked through a progressive selection of meanings intrinsically related to the constitution of stones, mystery is not a socially recognized quality of most objects. Indeed, the tendency of thinking in our culture is toward demystification of the material world, toward finding natural causes for what at first may appear inexplicable.

If, as it has been argued, language conveys meaning because words have sharable social implications, a correct reading of anagogical writing would depend upon an audience for whom some words potentially have unusual and mystical extensions of meaning. That is, only readers for whom the concept of matter contains the possibility of immanent spirit could recognize the spiritual implications of a word that, in normal usage, contains no such connotation. While it might be assumed within a Christian language community, for example, that the word *lamb* has the implication of 'sacrificed god,' it cannot be assumed that this secondary meaning is shared by the community at large. I am not suggesting here that no words in our language convey religious implications. This is observably untrue. I am contending that a religious extension of meaning, outside of specific cases, is usually unconventional, and since we arrive at ulterior meanings through a previous experience of a shared type, the absence of such convention may preclude understanding. Personal implications must be signaled in some other way.

It follows that a writer whose aim is to secure the recognition of a spiritual dimension—when she realizes, as O'Connor did, that she is addressing an audience that does not generally use language to imply the supernatural—must rely on techniques other than the normal ones for revealing implication. To answer the question posed earlier, one cannot use the word *stone* to imply the sacred unless a prior convention of holiness is associated with the word or unless one sets up other criteria in the text that indicate that a word is used in an unconventional or private manner. Wallace Stevens does this when he uses the word *rock* in "Form of the Rock in a Night Hymn." "The rock is the gray particular of man's life,/ The stone from which he rises up."[25] The poet directly states a special meaning for rock. Once the rather unspecific phrase "the gray particular of man's life" is understood, a simple substitution process can begin, in which further use of the word *rock* implies, not the conventional characteristics of the word, but the meaning that Stevens has indicated as operative for the duration of the poem.

Enough is known of O'Connor's sensitivity toward a presumedly ignorant and hostile audience to warrant the supposition that she understood the need for setting up particular conditions in the literal sense of her prose which would direct a reader's understanding from literal to unconventional ulterior meanings. Indeed, she was extraordinarily concerned with creating extreme and even violent effects in her stories. The specifics of her techniques will be discussed in Chapters Three through Six, but it should be noted that she was not certain she had successfully communicated her beliefs. "I don't believe that we shall have great religious fiction until we have again that happy combination of believing artist and believing society. Until that time, the novelist will have to do the best he can in travail with the world he has. He may find in the end that instead of reflecting the image at the heart of things, he has only reflected our broken condition."[26] As Chapter Two will show, this disparity between the assumptions of a religious writer and of an unbelieving society often became the focus of O'Connor's reflections on the requirements of art. "We forget that what is to us an extension of sight is to the rest of the world a peculiar and arrogant blindness."[27] Yet for her there was no question that the Christian point of view was the fuller and somehow more realistic appraisal of life, and given this conviction, her effort in writing was not to vindicate belief, but to make it apparent.

Being part of "the rest of the world," that is, part of O'Connor's lay readership, I share the artist's hesitance in proclaiming the success of her anagogical achievement. The "image at the heart of things" is very difficult to put into words. However, the purpose of this volume is not to discredit O'Connor's religious beliefs, but to separate the issues of belief and cognition in the reading of prose fiction. Given this concern, the question is not whether a reader wishes to know the ineffable, or whether he agrees with a specific formulation of its nature, but simply, whether the conventions of rendering employed by the artist compel him to see that an "added dimension" exists at all.

TWO

The Writer's Sense of Audience

I

In a rare and uncomfortable interview several years ago, there was a terse, acrid exchange between William Faulkner and Jean Stein:

> STEIN: Some people say they can't understand your writing even after they read it two or three times. What approach would you suggest for them?
>
> FAULKNER: Read it four times.[1]

Admittedly Faulkner cultivated an image of himself as ever quick on the draw and a dead shot, but his answer, given in the spirit of instant repartee, accurately represents his attitude toward the reading public: devil take the average man's literary understanding. Faulkner wrote from a sense of purpose that preceded and was independent of anyone else's apprehension of his work.

When such bold self-sufficiency marks a writer's intellectual stance, questions of artistic community become superfluous. But artists are not always indifferent to isolation. To the contrary, it has posed an openly conceded problem since novels have been written. In this country, Henry James spoke to the point when he compared his own felt solitude to the sense of community that presumably bolstered Hawthorne.[2] James's formulation of his difficulty has become a classic statement of the artist's predicament in a post-Christian era. His lament is not for the passing of specific doctrines, but for a lost community of belief. He recognized that the loss of shared assumptions implied a dilemma for the artist, who could no longer suppose that those he addressed understood his implicit norms for human conduct.

From the beginning of her writing career, Flannery O'Connor wrote as a loner, accepting what James found so unfortunate. For any writer, the lack of a community of shared belief inevitably results in an odd and fragmentary sense of his audience; but as a southern Catholic, O'Connor faced not only the isolation most artists experience, but an estrangement peculiar to a convinced Christian in a secular culture.[3] Although she disclaimed overt didacticism, the spiritual mainspring of her writing was clear to her: "I see from the standpoint of Christian orthodoxy. This means that for me the meaning of life is centered in our Redemption by Christ and what I see in the world, I see in its relation to that."[4]

Her critics came from two sides—the avowedly Christian and the agnostic in literary matters. O'Connor was acutely aware of both audiences, and in one sense her collection of occasional prose, *Mystery and Manners*, is an extended apology to one group or the other. Faulkner professed to think his readers of no account; Virginia Woolf found them an annoyance that she would rather ignore, for they held the novelist "in thrall to provide a plot, to provide comedy, tragedy, love interest."[5] O'Connor, by contrast, was haunted by them. "Success," she wrote to a friend, "means being heard. . . . You may write for the joy of it, but the act of writing is not complete in itself. It has its end in its audience."[6] Generally she weathered criticism with good grace, but she did not put it off silently; she joked and she answered back. Not that she anticipated changing the character of her work in consequence of adverse reactions, but she wanted the writing to be apprehended in the spirit of its conception, and she sensed, accurately, an initial resistance to the wild contours of the stories.

With Catholic audiences, O'Connor was anxious primarily to avoid the claim that the work was not positive or uplifting and that its mirror of depravity might corrupt the unsuspecting. Several essays in *Mystery and Manners* constitute O'Connor's answer to the demand that literature be used in the service of dogma. While they amply document her personal faith, it is clear that she resented this expectation.[7] To her it was misguided, and thus any criticism of her writing that issued from it proceeded on unsound critical ground.

It is not difficult to sympathize with her impatience at the implied imperative of such statements as: "Why not a positive novel based on the Church's fight for social justice, or the liturgical revival, or life in a seminary?" or "Would it not seem in order now for some of our younger men to explore the possibilities inherent in certain positive factors which make Catholic life and the Catholic position in this country increasingly challenging?"[8] As O'Connor rightly observes, these attitudes derive from a desire to supply the general needs of a lay Catholic readership. They are concerned with the image of the Church and with moral teaching; in them art is of less interest than utility.

O'Connor countered these directives most attentively, even though the natural reflex of her annoyance might have been to ignore them or to discredit her critics. She saw that her own aesthetic values were not self-evident to all Catholics; and in the interest of redefining the grounds for appreciating Catholic literature, as well as shaping public attitudes toward her own work, O'Connor answered her religious readers.

Her self-defense rested primarily on the authority of Thomas Aquinas.[9] The main point of her argument was to separate the concept of "Catholic novel" from "the rendering of Catholic life." In her opinion, the author's vision of life rather than the novel's subject identified a work of art as Christian. Consequently, the religious novelist's first aim was to represent reality adequately, not just the values and behavior of a selected cultural group. In this her reasoning echoed the thought of Jacques Maritain, a writer whose work she admired, who warned the artist not to compromise either the faith of personal life or the demands of art. "Do not separate your art from your faith," he advised, "but keep distinct what is distinct. Do not try to confuse forcibly what life joins so well. If you turn your aesthetic into an article of faith, you will spoil your faith. If you convert your devotion into a rule of artistic procedure, or if you turn your concern to edify into an artistic method, you will spoil your art." For Maritain it is not what the artist depicts that is important, but how he depicts it. "The essential question is not whether or not a novelist can portray this or that aspect of evil. The essential question is to what heights he will aspire to render his portrayal, and whether his art and his heart are pure enough and strong enough to render it without complicity. The more deeply the novel probes human misery, the more it demands superhuman virtues of the novelist." [10] Thus the representation of evil is not in itself reprehensible, for one kind of subject matter can be understood variously, according to the perspective from which it is viewed. Point of view, then, replaces specific content as the essential obligation of the Christian writer, and Maritain strongly implies that the only writer who can be a complete artist is the Christian who understands the potentials of men and can delineate human limitations in light of an ideal.

These ideas were clearly important to O'Connor, who claimed the freedom to represent any aspect of life that she observed. She was not alone in her enthusiasm. Because the writings of Maritain have influenced other novelists, it is useful to look at the ways in which two other Catholic writers, François Mauriac and Graham Greene, faced similar charges of portraying the sordidness of life with too much sympathy. Both countered these attacks from other Catholics by citing Maritain's observations about underlying perspective versus overt content and by explaining the artist's need for complete and disinterested rendering as an essential tool of his craft. The quality of a work of art, to them, depended on the sense of felt life that it created. To limit that sense of life arbitrarily to "good" or Christian behavior was to refuse representation to the greater part of the created universe. Mauriac even rationalized that Christianity was immanent in all of life. "There is no need to tamper with reality;" he wrote, "to describe modern man in all his misery is to reveal the chaos left in this world by the absence of God." [11]

These claims for freedom of expression backfired on occasion. André Gide, an agnostic commentator, accused Mauriac of being of the devil's party, of letting into his work "that reassuring compromise that allows one to love God without losing sight of Mammon." [12] His criticism occasioned Mauriac's publication of an essay "God and Mammon," in which he accepted Gide's observation ("I am probably more guilty than a man who is tugged both ways, who wants to write his books without missing heaven and to win without forgoing his books"); but he proceeded to justify himself anyway, remarking that God is revealed even in his apparent absence. [13] By the end of his writing career, however, Mauriac seems to have become far more pessimistic about the possibility of a marriage between faith and fiction. "If there existed anywhere a world of fiction which took account of eternity, I would still have recourse to it . . . Bernanos? Graham Greene? But all fiction, even when it does admit the active presence in this world of Grace, merely has the effect of cheapening a truth which is not the product of invention, and is beyond the power of words to communicate." [14] Moreover, he considered Christian art inevitably to be manipulative. Although he had previously maintained that the perspective of the writing could introduce a certain metaphysics into fiction without distorting accurate representation, he felt at this point that the novelist could do nothing but direct the development of his characters to a specific purpose. Where once he had explained the novelist's position as analogous to God's—in that both create and then allow their creations the freedom of self-determination—he finally discounted the analogy on the ground that character was never rendered independent of an author's purpose. Consequently, the novel could never be an authentic copy of reality, but, at most, a refraction of the world made through the particular concerns of each writer. He ended his career with the conflict between his faith and his art unresolved, even after major attempts throughout his life to reconcile them. Either a religious point of view must be articulated, with inevitable distortion or manipulation of craftsmanship, or one was left with an art devoid of identifiable conviction.[15] Implied values were insufficient. Mauriac was always vulnerable to the charge that by giving free reign to the dictates of both imagination and unbiased observation, he had effectively betrayed his faith.

Though he appears never to have felt the demands of the Church in the personal and tormented manner of his French contemporary, Graham Greene responded to similar accusations much as Mauriac had. His position is clearly stated in a letter to Elizabeth Bowen and V. S. Pritchett.

> If I may be personal, I belong to a group, the Catholic Church, which would present me with grave problems as a writer were I not saved by my disloyalty. If my conscience were as acute as M. Mauriac's showed itself to be in his essay "God and Mammon," I could not write a line. There are leaders of the Church who regard literature as a means to an end, edification.
>
> I am not arguing that literature is amoral, but that it presents a different moral, and the personal morality of an individual is seldom identical with the morality of the group to which he belongs. You remember the black and white squares of Bishop Blougram's chess board. As a novelist, I must be allowed to write from the point of view of the black square as well as the white: doubt and even denial must be given their chance of self-expression, or how is one freer than the Leningrad group?[16]

Greene avoided personal conflict by resisting immediately, and without apparent anxiety, the religious utility of fiction, even on the issue of perspective. By insisting that the point of view expressed in writing was uniquely his own, he entirely skirted the issue of didacticism. For him, the demands of art were thoroughly separate from the teachings of his faith, and it was only by open disregard for the Church that he could write at all. In this manner, he considered himself free from the accusations of immoral subject matter that so plagued Mauriac. In fact, he had no compunction about writing. "It is the genuine duty [of novelists] to awaken sympathetic comprehension in our readers—not only for our most evil characters, but for our smug, complacent, successful characters." [17]

The theme common to these discussions about the Catholic novelist's obligation is the artist's need for uninhibited expression. The need is acute, and the arguments can be seen as rationalizations for a freedom considered essential to craftsmanship. Like Mauriac and Greene, O'Connor asserted that "the Catholic novelist doesn't have to be a saint; he doesn't even have to be a Catholic; he does, unfortunately, have to be a novelist." Her subsequent arguments support this claim by encouraging Catholics to view creative independence as inherently good. She pointed out that talent is a gift with concomitant possibilities and limitations and that discrete exercise of talent depends upon working within boundaries that may or may not include Catholic teachings. "There is no excuse," she wrote, "for anyone to write fiction for public consumption unless he has been called to do so by the presence of a gift. It is the nature of fiction not to be good for much unless it is good in itself." [18]

Her sense of the writer's vocation as a calling echoes Mauriac's admission that for him writing expressed a deep and imperative need: he could not not write.[19] But Mauriac saw his need in very personal terms and his craft as fulfillment of a self that was far from perfect. Consequently, he was concerned with the ontology of art, with "purifying" his life in the interest of moral art, as if character traits could be directly transferred to the fiber of his work. Unlike this hesitant Frenchman, O'Connor seems to have redirected the issue of personal morality and writing to a concern for the aesthetics of the piece. When she discussed a work's "goodness," she spoke not of its moral effect or the quality of its source, but of characteristics intrinsic to the form of fiction. Balance, wit, accuracy of representation—the language of aesthetics—replaced ethical terminology in her descriptions, and in support of this inclination she observed with Thomas Aquinas that what is good in itself glorifies God.[20] None of Mauriac's self-doubt permeates her essays on the subject of Catholic art. In fact, when asked why she wrote, she once snapped, "Because I'm good at it," a remark that reminds us of one of her college essays, "Excuse Us While We Don't Apologize."[21] At no time was she simply a Catholic apologist. She seems to have been secure in her vocation and seriously dedicated to the exercise of a talent that was, as she saw it, bestowed on her. The concept of the God-given gift, of the writer as one chosen in the Old Testament manner, apparently settled questions of her own moral status with regard to her work. Beyond that, her essays constitute an implicit rejection of a more obvious obligation to the Church. To the extent that she achieved excellence in writing, she considered that she spoke for her faith; to the degree that she ordered and sharpened her prose, she testified to the order of all God's creation. In O'Connor's opinion, no dogma could possibly instruct this achievement, and thus it had no proper claim to benefit directly from her craftsmanship.[22] In effect, she joined Graham Greene in the assertion that a certain kind of disloyalty to the Church constituted the basis of her art; she would not alter her writing to accommodate immediate religious utility.

II

O'Connor's regard for the general reading public was, superficially, another instance of her disregard for Catholics. "The writer whose vocation is fiction sees his obligation as being to the truth of what can happen in life, and not to the reader—not to the reader's taste, not to the reader's happiness, not even to the reader's morals."[23] Reiterating the comments leveled at Catholic critics, she said that only the exigencies of art motivated and directed her writing. But to accept O'Connor's observation uncritically is to miss a central, disturbing contradiction in her self-evaluation. For it is obvious that she did write with a particular audience in mind. In the same way that her prose essays are delivered to either a Catholic or a non-Catholic audience and tailored accordingly, her fiction is discernibly shaped by concern for an imagined secular reader. She described her awareness graphically, as Miss Muffit might have described the spider: "When I sit down to write, a monstrous reader looms up who sits down beside me and continually mutters, 'I don't get it, I don't see it, I don't want it.' Some writers can ignore this presence, but I have never learned how. I know that I must never let him affect my vision . . . yet I feel I must make him see what I have to show, even if my means of making him see have to be extreme."[24]

As any rhetorician recognizes, his conceptualization of an audience will affect both the direction an argument will take and, to some degree, the significance that will be attributed to it. Like the rhetorician or orator, the writer of prose fiction manipulates to persuade and tries to establish premises that will serve as acceptable foundations for his argument. This is not to insist that fiction is reducible to a series of logically developed statements. It is not. But insofar as a writer aims to "make [the reader] see what [he has] to show," as O'Connor did, his intention is rhetorical and subject to analysis in those terms.

In light of O'Connor's careful insistence that she would not cater to the Church's suggested use of her talent, her sensitivity to the imagined demands of a non-Christian audience deserves attention. No group actually demanded anything of her, but to some extent any writer addresses an audience of his own making, a private and systemized construction. O'Connor's sense of these readers as a brooding and stupid presence shaped the course of her writing career and elicited from her a stronger sense of obligation than she ostensibly felt for Catholics. She admitted that her writing was done to particular effect, for the influence of ignorant minds, not just for the aestheticism she had previously cited as her own best motivation.

At the point when a critical reader of O'Connor's essays stops regarding the writer as she wanted to regard herself—as an aestheti-cian rather than a writer with a message—he can appreciate how many of her comments about craftsmanship are, in fact, discussions of methods for heightening rhetorical effect, particularly through exaggeration or distortion. She also wrote time and again of her orthodox perspective, of her evaluation of the religious climate in this country, and of the implications that this particular estrange-ment between reader and writer had for her as a prose artist. "The problem of the novelist who wishes to write about a man's encoun-ter with this God is how he shall make the experience, which is both natural and supernatural, understandable and credible to his reader. In any age this would be a problem, but in our own, it is a well-nigh insurmountable one. Today's audience is one in which re-ligious feeling has become, if not atrophied, at least vaporous and sentimental." Having identified the distance between her own the-ological and clearly articulated viewpoint and that which she as-sumed in her reader, and having surmised a general hostility toward her beliefs, she acknowledged the need for rhetoric. "The Catholic writer often finds himself writing in and for a world that is unpre-pared and unwilling to see the meaning of life as he sees it. This means frequently that he must resort to violent literary means to get his vision across . . . the images and actions he creates may seem distorted and exaggerated." [25]

O'Connor is never more specific. As a commentator on her own work, she is better able to locate problems than to discuss methods of dealing with them. This is certainly the case in "Novelist and Be-liever," where she wrote: "You can't have effective allegory in times when people are swept this way and that by momentary convic-tions because everyone will read it differently. You can't indicate moral values when morality changes with what is being done, be-cause there is no accepted basis of judgment. And you cannot show the operation of grace when grace is cut off from nature or when the very possibility of grace is denied, because no one will have the least idea of what you are talking about." [26] What *can* be said is left unspecified.

O'Connor, however, did at least allude to writing strategies. "Henry James wrote that the young woman of the future, though she would be taken out for airings in a flying machine, would know nothing of mystery or manners. James had no business to limit the prediction to one sex; otherwise, no one can very well disagree with him. The mystery he was talking about is the mystery of our position on earth, and the manners are those conventions which, in the hands of the artist, reveal that central mystery."[27] The key word is *conventions*. O'Connor wrote at a time when allegory, the traditional device for translating patterns of fictional action into an equivalent lattice of spiritual or moral significance, had become impossible. John Ruskin had been able to interpret *The Faerie Queene* with a simple substitution process: "The Redcrosse Knight (Holiness)...has Una (Truth) at his side, but presently enters the wandering wood and encounters the serpent Error."[28] Ruskin translated the narrative material into abstract terms. Character and setting were given consistent symbolic identification, and their conceptual relations were indicated by narrative action. He worked from fiction to supposed truths. But for O'Connor, the framework of communal religious assumption was almost aggressively absent, and, as she correctly appraised, no rules of transformation could function when the religious terms of the fictional equation were interpreted disparately or not at all. As early as 1852 Herman Melville had articulated a similar sense of moral fragmentation when he observed in *Pierre*, "Say what some poets will, Nature is not so much her own ever-sweet interpreter, as the mere supplier of that cunning alphabet, whereby selecting and combining as he pleases, each man reaches his own peculiar lesson according to his own peculiar mind and mood."[29] Flannery O'Connor had not only to render the physical world, but, denied allegory yet desiring to picture the "truths" of allegory, to discover an alternate set of conventions that would render a nonspecific religious dimension as well.

This is an interesting and difficult problem. O'Connor's aim was to define, in the language of fiction, an area of experience normally accessible through intuition and only to a select few. Not only did

she have to write without the assurance of a shared sensibility—in
the way one might describe a solo airplane flight to the uninitiated—but she intended to communicate that which the reader did
not know to exist—the movement of spiritual grace. She set for
herself the goal of alerting an ignorant and unreceptive audience to
the possibilities of the ineffable by employing traditions of usage
and conventions of embodiment more commonly reserved to signal typical, concrete experience. It was a problem encountered
previously and with distress by Mauriac, who asked: "But how is
one to describe the secret drama of a man who struggles to subdue
his earthly heritage, that drama which finds expression neither in
words nor gestures? Where is the artist who may dare to imagine
the processes and shifts of the great protagonist—Grace? . . . It is
the mark of our slavery and of our wretchedness that we can, without lying, paint a faithful portrait only of the passions." [30] O'Connor's answers were given primarily in her fiction rather than her
essays.

III

To imply, however, that O'Connor's essays are devoid of
technical discussions of fiction writing is misleading. Such comments in her work are meager, but they are to be found. In an essay,
"The Novelist and Free Will," she wrote, "I think the more a writer
wishes to make the supernatural apparent, the more real he has to
be able to make the natural world, for if the readers don't accept
the natural world, they'll certainly not accept anything else." [31]
Plainly she felt her starting point in fiction, her moment of common, undisputedly shared sympathy with her readers, to be in realistic narrative. Although O'Connor recognized that all novelists are
fundamentally seekers and describers of the real and that the realism of each novelist depends on his view of the ultimate reaches of
reality, *realism* in this volume will refer to the art of verisimilitude,
a convention of writing specifically recognizable in its skillful and
consistent imitation of the social, economic, and psychological aspects of human experience. [32] Realism avoids the vague and inex-

plicable in favor of rendering concretely both the life of the mind and the objective surface of human action. As such, it is the convention of a secular culture. It assumes no ulterior realities except those of human psychology, as characters mask their motives or specific knowledge from each other. The focus of the James novel, for example, is often the subtleties of social intercourse as they are encountered by a single intelligence. Even in those James stories where characters are haunted, and in which it initially seems feasible to postulate a supernatural dimension, the gods are shown to reside within the human skull, their power taken from unexamined recesses of mind that operate forcefully, though unconsciously. The "beast" in the jungle turns out to be no actual four-legged monster or winged demon, but the temerity of a man too egoistically preoccupied to engage in a proffered relationship with a woman. Even in *The Turn of the Screw*, where "ghosts" perceptibly alter the conduct of several persons, the existence of the supernatural is never objectively verified. Peter Quint and Miss Jessel may haunt the governess, but they may just as credibly be taken as extensions of hyperactive or sinister imagination. We are left with, at most, an ambiguity. To me, the more interesting reading searches out the deep structures of character that can adequately explain Flora, Miles, and the governess's superficially strange behavior.

So it is somewhat odd that O'Connor should align herself with the tradition of realism, since social, economic, and psychological explanations of human interaction were of secondary importance to her. When she did speak of a central concern in writing, it was often of "mystery" or an "added dimension" over and above literal reality. But reconsider the quotation from "The Novelist and Free Will," for it suggests that O'Connor considered realism not as an end but as a vehicle. It was the rhetorical base for a Christian argument, a starting point at which her essentially mystical intelligence could meet an imagined secular reader's demands for natural rendering.

To let O'Connor's comments about realistic writing stand as an unquestioned analysis of the parameters of her work would be to misconstrue both her aims and her achievements in prose. For she was a "realist of distances," a synthesizer of the common with the unusual and violent. Once again, use of grotesquery and distortion as writing techniques originated in a concern for manipulating an audience.

> The novelist with Christian concerns will find in modern life distortions which are repugnant to him, and his problem will be to make these appear as distortions to an audience which is used to seeing them as natural; and he may well be forced to take ever more violent means to get his vision across to this hostile audience. When you can assume that your audience holds the same beliefs you do, you can relax a little and use more normal means of talking to it; when you have to assume that it does not, then you have to make your vision apparent by shock—to the hard of hearing you shout, and for the almost blind you draw large and startling figures.[33]

In O'Connor's view, the grotesque was not only a consciously cultivated fictional strategy but was logically inevitable. Not only did she perceive a malformed world, but in response to the supposed blindness of those who considered the normal to be normal, she would exaggerate the deformity she herself saw. This hyperbole, the heightening of perversity and concentrated emphasis on violence, became a central rhetorical tool. "Of the nineteen stories . . . nine end in the violent death of one or more persons. Three others end in, or present near the end, physical assaults that result in bodily injury. Of the remaining seven, one ends in arson, another in the theft of a wooden leg, another in car theft and wife abandonment."[34] The other four leave their characters considerably shaken but alive. Each of the novels contains a murder and, taken together, they portray a wide range of lesser offenses, including rape, self-mutilation, vandalism, and police brutality. "Redemption is meaningless," O'Connor pointed out, "unless there is cause for it in the actual life we live, and for the last few centuries there has been operating in our culture the secular belief that there is no such cause."[35] It is reasonable to consider that the violent details were employed to ensure that no one could miss seeing humanity's weakness and consequent need for salvation.

Realism and the grotesque, then, are the two aspects of crafts-manship that O'Connor herself commented on. On the one hand she wrote that "fiction is an art that calls for the strictest attention to the real," implying the importance of accurately transcribing re-ality, while on the other hand she asserted that distortion and exag-geration were also fundamental to her style.[36] Although O'Connor saw no contradiction in this dual focus, I find such a marriage of technique disquieting. I assume Ruth Vande Kieft did too when she asked, "Is the distortion in the perspective or in what is per-ceived? . . . Does disruption come from the sense of distortion or of truth?"[37] Unless there is an implied norm, recognizing proportion or distortion in fiction can become problematic.

A reader who is not given a basis for judging conduct within a text will judge fictional events according to a pattern of expecta-tion drawn from his own experience. This does not mean that every individual considers his personal idiosyncrasies to be the measure of all human actions, but it does imply that people become ac-customed to a spectrum of conduct and that this range provides an implicit reference in judging the normality or strangeness of newly encountered behavior. To some extent, Flannery O'Connor real-ized this when she wrote in a letter that "people make a judgment of fanaticism by what they are themselves."[38] However, she also spoke repeatedly of her audience's limitations and "blind spots," implying that her readers' typical judgments about fanaticism or ex-treme behavior were bound to be wrong. Given O'Connor's assess-ment of audience response and her need to redirect it, one antici-pates that both her realism and hyperbole are used rhetorically, that a radical manipulation of the reader's judgment is being attempted.

It remains to determine the degree of rearrangement of reality and its effectiveness in O'Connor's portrayals. Are we to recognize in the deeds of lonely, sex-crazed evangelists, desperate, self-righteous farm widows, cripples, and drifters the sign of our own displacement? Do the freaks typical of O'Connor's fictive world make derogatory comment on the "normality" of our lives? Are we asked to identify with the weird experience charted in the stories, or conversely, to recognize in their eccentricity the record of eminently possible but definitely abnormal behavior?

O'Connor's nonfiction prose indicated that she wanted the reading experience to be a "descent through the darkness of the familiar world, where . . . [one] sees men as if they were trees walking." But again, to identify an author's motive is not to tribute him with successful or effective use of language. The question is not whether the author meant something by x utterance, but whether it is possible to construe a certain meaning from x. Even granting that O'Connor has rendered strange what we usually perceive as familiar, what use are we to make of this recognition? For a writer who admits openly that "what he sees on the surface will be of interest to him only as he can go through it into an experience of mystery itself," there is presumably further significance to overtly strange fictive behavior; but how do such meanings accrue?[39]

In her published essays O'Connor did not specifically address this problem. She was not offering advice to professional writers, nor was she communicating with creative friends, so it is not surprising that she avoided the technical and specific in favor of more general statements of purpose. Nonetheless, it is possible to identify writing tactics from reading the stories and novels and to discuss their effectiveness apart from O'Connor's commentary on her work.

At this point in the discussion, we know certainly that we are dealing with an author who recurrently anticipated audience reactions and played against attitudes and ignorance that she supposed were prevalent and conducive to certain patterns of reading responses. We know also that realism and grotesquery were two principal techniques used to manipulate awareness of the spiritual implications of human experience. But within the classifications "grotesque" and "realism," further discriminations are to be made. The chapters that follow specify what happens when an author's identifiable intention is conjoined with a not fully acknowledged sensitivity to audience reactions, and locate, regardless of motivation, the meanings that the language of narration allows a reader to recognize and share. Specifically, the aim of each chapter is to investigate a single rhetorical technique. In O'Connor's fiction, several rhetorical strategies may operate simultaneously, or one maneuver may subsume two kinds of rhetoric. An allusion, for example, may also be grotesque. But for the purposes of clarity, the categories considered here are isolated, and consequently, their order in the essay is somewhat arbitrary. The general discussion, however, progresses from the fictional situations in which O'Connor's rhetorical manipulations are most devious, leaving spiritual connections to be inferred, if at all, from ambiguous evidence, to those narratives that include sufficient "telling" to make values unequivocally clear.

THREE

Extensions of the Grotesque

I

When Sister Kathleen Feeley went down to Milledgeville, Georgia, she met one of Flannery O'Connor's townspeople. As
Feeley tells the anecdote, the woman "told me that she knew Flannery O'Connor and her mother and often ate at the Sanford House
where the O'Connor mother and daughter usually lunched. But she
added, 'I never went near her because I didn't want her to put me in
one of those stories.'"[1]

The woman's misapprehension was in some ways shrewd. She
knew enough about her hometown storyteller to realize that
O'Connor's work was intensely local in idiom and manners and that
what derived from that parochial southern focus was seldom pleasant. "Why don't she write about some nice people?" was probably a
typical neighborly response, but behind its naïveté lay a truth important to more considered criticism: the confused reception of the
work did not stem from anyone's failure to recognize the grotesque, but from the inability to ascribe useful motivation to this
concentrated focus on the maimed and misshapen.[2]

In some respects, these misunderstandings are predictable, for
grotesque writing elicits response through a complicated and often
uneasy balance of comedy and terror. It undercuts a reader's poten-

tially sympathetic identification with horrible experience by ironic or humorous rendering, suggesting implicitly that the categories which normally apply to our world view are no longer applicable. In this situation, confusion may well be rife, and laughter then becomes the reader's best defense against a world rendered strange beyond recognition; it affords relief from the tension of finding meaning gone unexpectedly askew. Wolfgang Kayser observed that the grotesque instills the fear of life rather than the fear of death. Such a consideration may have led Thomas Mann to dub the grotesque "the genuine anti-bourgeois style," the natural procedure of verbal protest against a too-easy faith in the integrity of established social institutions. In addition, Nathan Scott has contended, "All the great charismatic seers of modern literature from Baudelaire to Kafka and from Pirandello to Faulkner, in one way or another have wanted us to understand that we are lost in a dark wood and that in this maze, what is least trustworthy is the common, the immediate, the familiar."[3] If we bear all this in mind, we can see the grotesque as an appropriate technical approach for any critic of contemporary values, particularly when we recognize that character or situation in fiction is grotesque only in relation to something else. As with the recognition of any rhetorical device, a grotesque extremity of diction or rendering depends for effect upon some sense of what constitutes a normal or undeflected mode of perception and narration. Thus it can be assumed that the writer of the grotesque has in mind an alternative by which he recognizes and renders distortion. A reader's determination of this unstated standard of measurement allows the grotesque mode to furnish, in addition to explicit criticism, an implicit vision of an unexpressed potential.

The process of deducing the ideal that identifies the grotesque as a distortion or exaggeration is a special case in which inference proceeds by reasoning from an effect to a cause. When this problem occurs in fiction, it entails determining what conditions in the text serve as sufficient grounds for inferring a standard. Need there be a literal portrayal of balance and proportion? May the writer assume that his readers already have such a standard and play against that expectation, or can norms be otherwise implied, though not expressly stated?

Flannery O'Connor addressed this problem when she admitted that a Christian writer may find "that instead of reflecting the image at the heart of things, he has only reflected our broken condition." Comic distortion can easily estrange a reader from the fictional life portrayed, but even in O'Connor's mind, moving an audience from the recognition of imperfection to perception of the norm itself remained problematic. Her own perspective was clear. In "Some Aspects of the Grotesque in Southern Fiction," she wrote, "To be able to recognize a freak, you have to have some conception of the whole man, and in the South, the general conception of man is still, in the main, theological."[4] It should be recalled that Jacques Maritain was also of the opinion that the only writer who could be a complete artist was the Christian who understood the potentials of men and could delineate human limitations in light of that religious ideal.

With this concern, as with others, Feeley has done an excellent job of disclosing the particular impetus that O'Connor's reading gave to her intellectual development. We know from Feeley's research that Mircea Eliade again influenced O'Connor's thinking about the grotesque. In Eliade's book, *Patterns of Comparative Religion*, O'Connor marked two passages: "This setting apart sometimes has positive effects; it does not merely isolate, it elevates. Thus ugliness and deformity, while marking out those who possess them, at the same time make them sacred" and "Perfection in any sphere is frightening, and this sacred or magic quality of perfection may provide an explanation for the fear that even the most civilized societies seem to feel when faced with a genius or a saint. Perfection is not of this world. . . . The same fear . . . applies to everything alien, strange, new." She remarked to herself in the margins, "The grotesque is naturally the bearer of mystery, is dangerous."[5] We can surmise from these remarks and notations the author's probable line of reasoning: from a theological perspective, with the life of Christ as a standard, normal human life (that is, the pattern of activities, thoughts, and expectations that are socially condoned) is severely inadequate. Given that the normal is "freakish" in this eternal perspective, the problem for the Christian novelist is to emphasize or set apart normal character by the ugliness or deformity that Eliade suggested to be simultaneously fascinating and repulsive.

While there is a certain logic to this reasoning, there is also a peculiar arrogance to it; for assuming that one's own religion provides the only norms for recognizing the shortcomings of human endeavor is unwarranted. The grotesque does indeed disturb categories of the normal evaluating mind, but it does not necessarily imply that the unstated standard for recognizing proportion is Christian. A covert vision of unrealized human potential can arise from social, economic, or purely idiosyncratic norms. It is not only the Catholic novelist who can insist, as O'Connor did, that "what he sees at all times is fallen man perverted by false philosophies," but any writer or thinker who can imagine a better world than he experiences.[6] O'Connor's diction—"fallen man," "false philosophies"—suggests her particular religious bent, but W. B. Yeats, in another country, another era, with a philosophy peculiarly his own, remarked similarly, "I . . . am still bewildered and still vexed, finding it a poor and crazy thing that we who have imagined so many noble persons cannot bring our flesh to heel." [7]

From this we see that the inevitable result of a secular perspective is not necessarily the elevation of relative values to the level of the absolute, as O'Connor feared, for values can be considered relatively bad or relatively good, without claiming for these temporal visions the authority of absoluteness.[8] O'Connor's insistence that the religious have access to the only true concept of the "whole man" manifests the absolutist Christian's difficulty in granting humanity any goodness or decency of outlook, short of complete "salvation." In the end, her belief that there was "no other perspective by which [her stories] could have been written" was a blindness that led to ambiguity in many textual situations.[9] For, as we shall see in discussing specific texts, it is possible to infer a variety of norms in response to an encounter with the grotesque; or, in the absence of adequate guidelines, it may be impossible to see in the fiction anything more than humanity's broken condition.

II

"Is the distortion in the perspective or in what is perceived?" Ruth Vande Kieft's inquiry about O'Connor's stories is both an intriguing and a misleading question. As it is formulated, it assumes that there is a world "out there" to which the stories refer, and it suggests that the teller of the tales has one of two procedures: she either distorts the proportion of the world or writes with fidelity about what must be universally recognized as deformity.

Actually the texts do not seem neatly classifiable. Several of the stories focus on personalities and events decidedly outside the range of typical experience. The stories of Hazel Motes, the self-mutilating anti-Christ preacher; of Mr. Shiftlet, who marries and then abandons a thirty-year-old idiot woman in exchange for a rattletrap car; of sideshow freaks and cripples—all achieve their fascination and shock through choice of a particularly disquieting subject matter. In other cases, the core of the story is the seemingly benign experience of daily life—a visit to the doctor, running a small farm, riding a bus—in which the familiar becomes, in O'Connor's hands, a source of fear and distrust. O'Connor resorted both to bizarre subject matter and to a distended perspective on the ordinary with equally disturbing results.

"Good Country People," an example of the former tendency, is written with the focus on a disturbing encounter between two morally and physically maimed individuals.

> She smiled, looking dreamily out on the shifty landscape. She had seduced him without even making up her mind to try. "How?" she asked, feeling that he should be delayed a little.
> He leaned over and put his lips to her ear. "Show me where your wooden leg joins on," he whispered.
> The girl uttered a sharp little cry and her face instantly drained of color. The obscenity of the sugges-

tion was not what shocked her. As a child she had sometimes been subject to feelings of shame but education had removed the last traces of that as a good surgeon scrapes for cancer; she would no more have felt it over what he was asking than she would have believed in his Bible. But she was as sensitive about the artificial leg as a peacock about his tail. No one ever touched it but her. She took care of it as someone would his soul, in private and almost with her own eyes turned away. "No," she said.

"I known it," he muttered, sitting up, "you're just playing me for a sucker."

"Oh no no!" she cried. "It joins on at the knee. Only at the knee. Why do you want to see it?"

The boy gave her a long, penetrating look. "Because," he said, "it's what makes you different. You ain't like anybody else." [10]

The seduction of Joy-Hulga Hopewell is probably one of the most bizarre representations of intimacy in our recent literature. Begun as a crippled atheist's attempt to jar a young Bible salesman out of his naïveté, the love scene turns with dark irony into the tale of a jaded woman overcome by a cynicism and nihilism greater than her own. Although it is an old story of the fox and the chicken, of the trickster cunningly outwitted, there is no surprised delight at the outcome. The issues of good and evil are obscure, the result of the "rape" too peculiarly jarring, the characters too distantly rendered at the point of greatest vulnerability to effect a pleasurable sense of the tables turned.

In part, the grotesque tenor of this scene derives from a stark incongruity. The exchange in the country hayloft is at once stocked with the clichés of first love—hot breathing, sticky lips, awkward kisses, the requisite "proof" of love—and with responses totally alien even to uninitiated lovemaking. Manley Pointer's attempt at intimacy is hesitantly initiated with the question, "You ever ate a chicken that was two days old?" Hulga's concession to the conventions of dating is putting some Vapex on the collar of her dirty

T-shirt. Their conversation always borders on the ludicrous, and
Hulga responds to Manley's embraces with strange ideas of tender-
ness and candor. "'You poor baby,' she murmured. 'It's just as well
you don't understand,' and she pulled him by the neck, face down,
against her. 'We are all damned,' she said, 'but some of us have taken
off our blindfolds and see that there's nothing to see.' ... She lifted
his head and looked him in the eye. 'I am thirty years old,' she said.
'I have a number of degrees'" (287–88).

   Although the expected setup of the first date is here, the preoccupied and driven characters who play out the melodrama offset
any sentimentality. Were it not for the theft of Hulga's wooden leg,
the story might be read on the level of simple farce—an author's
play with the overworked conventions of country love. The leg's
loss, however, is accomplished by a devastating irony: Manley, the
apparently innocent victim, turns sadist; and since the wooden leg
possesses the only obliquely identifiable value in Hulga's sour life,
the action breaks through her detached and ironic self-image, leaving her defenseless for the first time in the narrative. The source of
Hulga's previous aloofness and condescension has become the vehicle of her greatest vulnerability. This action is a masterful ploy, an
unobjectionably executed reversal, one of the finest and yet strang-
est enactments of awakening in the O'Connor canon. Grotesqueness is recognized because the rape plays against expectations.
What is lost is not virginity; yet the weird violation—a wooden leg
unjoined and stolen—carries a sense of shame and importance that
is probably more pronounced because of its uniqueness.

   "Good Country People" is one of the several stories that Flannery
O'Connor chose to interpret publicly. She, too, realized that the accumulated meanings of Hulga's wooden leg moved the tale of
courtship from the level of low joke to something more expansive
and gripping. "The reader learns how the girl feels about her leg,
how her mother feels about it, and how the country woman on the
place feels about it; and finally by the time the Bible salesman
comes along, the leg has accumulated so much meaning that it is, as
the saying goes, loaded." In the author's view, Hulga's mutilated ex-

terior self is a sign of her unrecognized spiritual malaise, and the theft of the leg "reveal[s] her deeper affliction to her for the first time." The technique is that of the unadorned symbol—wooden leg = wooden soul—in which a physical aberration indicates or points to a less apparent spiritual deficiency. Because the description of the phenomenal world (the crippled leg) contains implications of human character (the maimed soul), the progression of the narrative on the level of observable action and response serves to discredit an analogous abstract trait: Hulga's belief in "nothing but her own belief in nothing." [11] Her defeat thus occurs on two levels, for she is both literally and emotionally disabled.

In this instance, the grotesque has, through significant association, the useful and recognizable function of identifying an analogous interior deformity. If the purpose of the narration is simply to uncover this "deeper affliction," then the story is unambiguously successful. If, however, the meaning we attach to the narrative events must account for the surrounding conditions of the "rape" —the character of Manley Pointer and the two women whose observations frame the picnic in the hayloft—then unanswered questions remain, because the rape scene contains apparently contradictory implications. Hulga is defeated by someone who holds the very philosophical position that she has claimed to espouse: "'And I'll tell you another thing, Hulga,' he said, using the name as if he didn't think much of it, 'you ain't so smart. I been believing in nothing ever since I was born!'" (291). This circumstance qualifies any outright condemnation of Hulga's philosophy, for we deduce from the hayloft scene, not that the woman's attitude was ineffectual, but that she did not fully believe it. In its unexpected violence, the rape disclosed a philosophic posture assumed at least partially for effect; it indicated to Hulga the full implications of nihilism— that nothing, including the prosthetic leg that accounts for her uniquely dour self-image, has value. The anxiety that shakes this crippled woman at the end of the narrative can be accounted for by her recognition of the bleakness of unprincipled human conduct as well as by an insight into her own lack of self-knowledge. Both the crippled personality and the action which forcibly awakens that personality are grotesque. The mock love scene achieves its unnerving effect from a compilation of perversities.

Hulga's responses in this scene are rendered with a deliberately controlled coolness. O'Connor's matter-of-fact delineation of idiosyncrasy in the face of affliction, here and throughout the text, is itself a source of grotesque effect. As in *The Violent Bear It Away*, significant aspects of personality have been revealed from the perspective of other characters. Mrs. Hopewell describes her daughter thus: "She went about all day in a six-year-old skirt and a yellow sweat shirt with a faded cowboy on a horse embossed on it. She thought this was funny. Mrs. Hopewell thought it was idiotic and showed simply that she was still a child. She was brilliant but she didn't have a grain of sense. It seemed to Mrs. Hopewell that every year she grew less like other people and more like herself— bloated, rude, and squint-eyed" (276).

This conscious exploitation of the peculiarities of character prohibits sympathetic response toward the disabled, and is equally effective in alienating the personalities of those without obvious handicaps. Mrs. Hopewell and Mrs. Freeman, the stock characters of a shabbily decent rural South, are rendered flatly, their personalities distilled into a set of banal preoccupations, their gestures and responses reduced and mechanized by O'Connor's sparse, biased description. Mrs. Freeman, for example, becomes like a truck. "Besides the neutral expression that she wore when she was alone, Mrs. Freeman had two others, forward and reverse, that she used for all her human dealings" (271). And the conversation of the two women becomes a catalog of platitudes. "'It's some that are quicker than others.' 'Everybody is different,' Mrs. Hopewell said. 'Yes, most people is,' Mrs. Freeman said. 'It takes all kinds to make the world.' 'I always said it did myself'" (273). "'Well, it takes all kinds of people to make the world go 'round,' Mrs. Hopewell said. 'It's very good we aren't all alike.' 'Some people are more alike than others,' Mrs. Freeman said" (282). While the two older ladies initially provide graphic contrast to Hulga and explain, through their insistent inanity, her aloof and disdainful posture, the Bible salesman explodes all the cripple's surface pretension, reducing her to the same stale perceptions that she had condemned in her mother. "Aren't you," she murmured, "aren't you just good country people?" (290).

In all respects, the story is extreme. The predominant social milieu of Mrs. Hopewell and Mrs. Freeman, the estrangement of the cripple, the base deception of the Bible salesman are all exaggerations of life. O'Connor once commented on her use of grotesque character in a letter to James Farnham. "Essentially the reason why my characters are grotesque," she explained, "is because it is the nature of my talent to make them so. To some extent the writer can choose his subject; but he can never choose what he is able to make live." [12] But the life recorded is rendered in weird configuration; caricatured personalities act out a drama of unexamined inner compulsions, while another grotesque action breaks with sudden irrationality into the once familiar world. While it is a narrative of extremes, the extremes exist apart from any radical tension between opposites. This is not a story of salvation and damnation, not an exploration of order versus chaos, for the grotesqueness of one character is revealed through the observation of yet another grotesque character. Cumulatively they define a human landscape with no respite from the absurd. It is certain that the behavior noted is evidence of the imperfection of life as we know it; but since the alternatives of nihilism, irritating platitude, and general inanity are not illustrated, we are left to secure our own estimate of proportioned and sane human conduct.

In "Good Country People" the alienating or destructive effect of the grotesque has been masterfully engineered, but the grounds for construing a specifically Christian idea of "the whole man" are not adequately developed. It is possible to surmise what is wrong in the fictional situation—that nihilism is self-limiting and that what at first appears to be the intellectually superior perspective in the text is itself insufficient. But what would be a viable point of view in an encounter with Manley Pointer? If anything, the story levels all philosophies, including potentially, the Christian one, for there is no

indication that the absurd can be anticipated or explained by anyone. This in itself is a remarkable achievement, a darkly humorous
and awful study of the violent disruption of habitual patterns of
thought. It offers a markedly derogatory evaluation of philosophic
systems without suggesting a perspective that could explain and
thereby limit or contain irrational experience. In this instance, ex-
ploding the myth of rational control, the negative purpose, is all
that stands as a safely deduced authorial intention. It is a laudable
achievement, but one attributable as well to William Faulkner,
Franz Kafka, or any of the other "great charismatic seers" of modern
literature, not simply to the Christian artist.

III

In O'Connor's stories about freaks, the narrative is grotesque because the characters live outside the boundaries of customary experience. Not many Manley Pointers, Hulga Hopewells,
or Hazel Moteses populate the normal reaches even of our imagina-
tions. But Mrs. Turpin, Mrs. May, and Mrs. Cope are types of women
almost painfully familiar. In spite of O'Connor's flippant defensive-
ness about ordinary life in the South ("I have found that anything
that comes out of the South is going to be called grotesque by the
Northern Reader, unless it is grotesque, in which case it is going
to be called realistic"), their southern characteristics are not the
source of their peculiarity.[13] In these cases, when the experience
rendered is easily imaginable, we can identify any ensuing distortion with the mode of narrative presentation rather than with that
which is set forth.

In O'Connor's imaginary world, we find no families and neigh-
bors with a common, albeit fictive, history and locale. O'Connor's
South has no equivalent of Yoknapatawpha County to provide links
in time, place, and custom between one narrative and the next. Setting is not defined cumulatively but by recurrence of types—alienated parents and children, farm employers and employees, small-
farm widows, intellectuals, and fanatical evangelists. They act out
their personal dramas in a common milieu, but without knowledge

of each other. Related by similarity of predicament rather than accident of proximity, the characters tell us that the author was more
concerned with certain archetypal patterns of private experience
than with depiction of specific social situations. As O'Connor observed, "I'm interested in the old Adam. He just talks southern because I do." [14]

We have, then, an imaginative world which is southern in superficial tenor, but which renders, through repetition of social types, experiences at least imaginatively common to us all. Mrs. Cope is a
self-righteous farm widow visited by three young city boys. Mrs.
May is a self-righteous farm widow who has problems with live-
stock, children, and hired help; Mrs. McIntyre is a self-righteous
widow who has to deal with tensions created by the life-styles and
expectations of her various farmhands. Ruby Turpin visits her doctor; Julian Chestny takes his mother to town on a bus. Without exception, the characters and experiences rendered place these stories within a sphere of recognizably normal existence; with equal
uniformity, these customary experiences are radically interrupted.
The unexpected violence in these stories can be easily recognized
as grotesque, but we should remember that O'Connor's purpose
was not to further her reader's recognition of violence but to make
them reevaluate realistic behavior. She wrote, "The freak in modern
fiction is usually disturbing to us because he keeps us from forget-
ting that we share his state. The only time he should be disturbing
to us is when he is held up as a whole man." [15] With the purpose of
rendering the familiar strange, of ensuring that the normal man appear as a partial, incomplete creature, she undertook to recount
tales of "typical" southern farm life. In this situation, it is important
to ask what technical strategies allowed her to effect a reversal of
wonted reading responses?

In "Good Country People," O'Connor rendered the bizarre world
of Hulga Hopewell in the flat tones of the mundane, making of
deformity a slack and understated habit. She could also work in an
antithetic mode, giving to the commonplace a sense of unvoiced
terror. In "A Circle in the Fire," the farm becomes a landscape of

intense psychic confrontation where even eating and ordinary sociability assume nervous undertones. As in many O'Connor stories,
the central event is a disaster, in this case, the conflagration of Mrs.
Cope's woods. But the significance of destruction is measured by
the tension that precedes it. Thus it is at least partially a narrative
about a woman's tightly controlled fear finding its proper object,
for Mrs. Cope's unacknowledged and suppressed anxiety about the
future anticipates the catastrophe. By the same token it is also the
story of an enlightenment, and Mrs. Cope's lesson about her limited
ability to own or control the environment initiates her into a community of suffering.

There are numerous ways to depict human limitations in fiction.
This particular story is made grotesque by O'Connor's exposure of
the anxiety and tension underlying a seemingly tranquil world. This
incongruity grows from a juxtaposition of weird preoccupations
and simple tasks of living, the combination of simple statements and
a strained mode of delivery, and, consistently, from the reader's implicit comparison between the characters and his own concept of
what is fitting behavior. Mrs. Pritchard, Mrs. Cope, and "the child"
collectively breach the expected proprieties of country living. The
child, for example, is excessively ugly and disagreeable. Conversation occurs not as an exchange but as a dual monologue, the dron-
ing repetition of singular obsessions. Mrs. Pritchard punctuates the
gardening session with reflections on the improbable and morbid
condition of a pregnant woman encased in an iron lung. Ignoring
the uncomfortable implications of the anecdote, Mrs. Cope speaks
unnaturally rapidly and with a suspect energy about her good fortune, while working "at the weeds and nut grass as if they were an
evil sent directly by the devil to destroy the place." [16] The continued narrative shows this to be a significant preoccupation and a
telling mode of behavior (Mrs. Cope's Negroes are also "as destructive and impersonal as the nut grass"). Through the repetition of
this gesture O'Connor finds an objective expression of anxiety; the
fierce digging gradually reveals an internal restlessness and Mrs.

Cope's desire to limit or contain the natural world, to have life con-
ducted only in the terms sanctioned by her will.

By the time the three city boys come to "visit" Mrs. Cope, the
compilation of significant details and the suggestion of unwarranted
behavior have undermined the normal surface of the countryside.
Significantly Mrs. Cope associates these youths with the nut grass,
and their antics awaken in her a more extreme version of the unacknowledged but gnawing fear. They are possessed of independent wills that counter hers, and they evade her attempts to control
them. "'I cannot have this,' Mrs. Cope said and stood at the sink
with both fists knotted at her sides. 'I cannot have this,' and her expression was the same as when she tore at the nut grass" (186).

We have, then, a portrait of a woman maintaining self-control and
the semblance of normal life while in fact struggling against an irrational feeling of being pursued and threatened. This anxiety is further evoked by the descriptions of a stolid and menacing landscape;
nature is as consistent a presence as any human being and is given
its own direction and sense of purpose. "The blank sky looked as if
it were pushing against the fortress wall [of trees]" (176). "The sun
. . . was swollen and flame colored and hung in a net of ragged cloud
as if it might burn through any second and fall into the woods"
(184). "The sun burned so fast that it seemed to be trying to set
everything in sight on fire . . . the grass was an unusual green as if it
were turning to glass" (184–85). By the time the city boys set fire
to the woods, their behavior is seen as reprehensible, but it is not
unexpected. Mrs. Cope's fear of fire operates in the fiction as a self-
fulfilling prophecy; the description of the landscape, which can
only look "as if" it might be the agent of holocaust, has encouraged
the anticipation of disaster. Thus the woman who was thankful for
her good fortune finds that she is not exempt from suffering.

In Mrs. Cope's reaction, in her "new misery," we find evidence of
the fate doled out to so many O'Connor characters, an example of
O'Connor's "fix 'em good and proper" attitude toward the self-
righteous. The moment of the woman's defeat, the point of her con-

scious entry into a situation not mitigated by wealth, social position, or a constructed self-image, would provide a lucid, satisfying
closure to this vignette, but O'Connor does not end with the focus
on Mrs. Cope. Instead, she switches the narrative away from the
personal revelation back to the source of enlightenment, and presumably to something more: "She [the child] stood taut, listening,
and could just catch in the distance a few wild, high shrieks of joy as
if the prophets were dancing in the fiery furnace, in the circle the
angels had cleared for them" (193). In this last instance, the author
plays once more with the effects of incongruity. While the grotesque was recognizable through an implicit comparison to our
concept of normal life in a given situation, the concluding allusion
to the prophets calls attention to itself because of its unexpected
contrast to the texture of the preceding fictional events: in no other
actions have there been even indirect biblical overtones. Since it
is not possible to derive the meaning of this allusion internally
through patterns, that is, by finding the similarities of circumstance
that give rise to such reference, the text itself suggests the possible
relevance of external information.

The allusion here is to the story of three Old Testament prophets
who were protected from burning in "a fiery furnace." As the tale is
told in the book of Daniel, Nebuchadnezzar, king of Babylon, constructed a singular and exotic image of a new god and required that
his subjects worship it. Three men—Shadrach, Meshach, and Abednego—took exception to these orders, maintaining their allegiance
to a hidden God, that is, to the God of the Hebrew people, who has
no image. In punishment for their nonconformity, Nebuchadnezzar
ordered them burned alive, taunting as he commanded their death
that such an invisible deity should prove his worth against the all
too tangible flames.[17] The irony of the story derives from God's pro-
tection; through his tale, the biblical writer has effectively commented on the efficacy of faith in the unseen.

Does O'Connor's allusion to this incident, coming strategically at
the end of the story, require that we reread her text in light of this
new information? We can take as a hypothesis that she had this re-

reading in mind. Proceeding with an inquiry about the dynamics of creating secondary levels of meaning in a text, we use the incongruity of allusion as a clue to search out, through selective exclusion, points of comparison between Mrs. Cope's southern farm and the distant biblical setting. Mrs. Cope is plagued by three boys who refuse to behave. Nebuchadnezzar finds three of his citizens intransigent. In both situations there is attempted destruction by fire. Is O'Connor's protagonist, by virtue of these parallel circumstances, to be identified with Nebuchadnezzar and the boys with Shadrach, Meshach, and Abednego? In my opinion, the only occasion when such a rereading is valid is when the literal text seems incomplete as it is presented and when a complete parallelism of incident can account for each of the details of the literal story. In this case, the parallelism is, at best, fragmentary, the comparison valid only as long as it is not scrutinized. In one case, the three prophets speak explicitly for their God; the fire is directed at them as Nebuchadnezzar's punishment. It can also be said that the miracle in the furnace effects to some degree the spiritual awakening of the king. In the O'Connor story, the boys have no message; the destruction appears to be gratuitous or at best the result of a deeply harbored resentment of the poor against the materially privileged. The most suggestive key to their behavior is their remark, "Man, Gawd owns them woods and her too" (186); but the fire is set not in consequence of that observation but in response to their own desire to claim the land: "It don't belong to nobody. It's ours" (192). The supposed prophets are not threatened; they have instead another victim in mind.

It can be said, then, that the boys have fulfilled the role of the prophets without themselves having the attributes of prophets. Although they are in some sense the agents of awakening, indicating the fallacy of Mrs. Cope's moral scheme and the difficulty of maintaining a "thankful" posture in the midst of misfortune, they are themselves evil. The destruction effects enlightenment while being itself reprehensible. This situation of concealed and unrecognized evil pitted against explicit evil creates a morally ambiguous conclusion and prevents reading the entire text in terms of the narrative in Daniel. The city boys simply do not represent a positive moral stance; they do not illustrate in action the alternative to the king's false god. An aura of mysterious significance is added to the story by this allusion, but the feeling of religion is in a sense borrowed. The allusion is not entirely inappropriate, but appearing without previous signals in a story that achieves an independently satisfactory closure, it appears as an attempt to "tack on" a significance that is as gratuitous as the boys' play with matches.[18]

IV

The narratives considered in this section illustrate two approaches to the technique of grotesque writing. In "Good Country People," the author exploits a macabre subject matter; "A Circle in the Fire," achieves its impact through deliberate exaggeration of commonplaces and a juxtaposition of incongruous elements. Regardless of the individual technical emphases, both texts disturb by accenting the shifty foundation of the immediate and familiar. Life is not to be assumed; it is to be feared. There is an underlying horror in our daily habits. In no case does O'Connor attempt to mitigate or explain that horror.

But these need not be the only modes of the grotesque, as Sherwood Anderson demonstrated. In his writing he created a similar sense of frightening and oppressive life, but he manipulated his readers' sympathy by expanding insights. This is especially true of *Winesburg, Ohio*, which Anderson initially called "The Book of Grotesques." Although he had a very private understanding of *grotesque* as a distortion ensuing from personal obsession with truth, his aim was to make disorders of character apparent and to expose and thereby explain the roots of aberrant behavior.[19] For example, Louise Bentley in "Godliness" is presented initially as a shrewish wife and negligent mother, but the narrative proceeds to disclose the tensions and frustrations of an isolated adolescence, which account for her peculiarities, and further, to connect this one woman's predicament with what Anderson takes to be a more general human situation—the inability of language to convey the dark, inchoate longings of the individual for wider community.

As far as we can tell from the text, Anderson's aim is to elicit our sympathy, to counter our stereotyped judgments of strange behavior by giving that behavior understandable roots in earlier and possibly traumatic experience. It is a method that maximizes a reader's identification with the portrayed fictional life. O'Connor, on the other hand, was concerned not with the antecedents of behavior but with its consequences. Her manifest intention, like Anderson's, was to discredit the normal evaluations of the reader, but she worked by restricting the possibility of sympathy rather than expanding or deepening it. Predictably, the results of such distancing were not only judgment—that is, the perception of dangers inherent in the superficially banal—but alienation, the reader's conviction that the self could not be reflected in the observed distortions of her fictional situations. This accounts in part for the reactions of O'Connor's townspeople, those who were afraid to know her for fear of being transformed in the fiction in some crude and demeaning way. It was not an entirely unfounded fear, for her tendency was both to render the mean and to demean in rendering. In part, the tenor of this writing can be explained as the expression of a natural bent, one that was displayed in O'Connor's earliest creative efforts—the satirical cartoons done for her college publications. O'Connor chose her subject matter, but she claimed, and I think correctly, that she could not choose what she could "make live." The informing spirit of her work was in a final sense inexplicable, for who can account for the gift of pointed caricature? But on another level, O'Connor perceived the grotesque to be particularly applicable to her point of view. Underlying the exaggerations and selection of weird incident in the fiction was the same belief that shaped Mauriac's thoughts on his craft—that God is revealed even in his absence.[20]

To examine this assumption is fundamental to the study of a writer who constructed her stories to have a calculated effect upon an audience. For her end is achieved in this instance only if the grotesque confers inevitably and specifically a sense of what is missing or of what has caused an observable deformity.

Although O'Connor imagined her typical reader to be an agnostic with regard to literary matters, she seems to have misjudged her audience's ability to understand the depraved behavior in her fiction to be the direct result of a godless world; for we can infer the lack of a specific dimension of life only if we know that dimension to exist or if we have had previous experience of it. It would seem that O'Connor predicated her fictional strategies on personal assumptions that her readers, by her own admission, did not share with her. Furthermore, I suspect that she did not fully evaluate the implications of her distorted rhetoric. As I understand it, grotesque writing of this type implicitly creates the necessity of judgment. The reader must either reject the point of view of writing that designates his everyday world to be suspect, or in accepting the authorial voice, he must reject his own previous cast of mind, which saw Mrs. Hopewell, Mrs. Cope, Mrs. Turpin, for examples, as normal. This is significant because it is limiting. Rather than creating an expansion of insight, as Anderson's stories do, O'Connor's stories suggest a restructuring of it, the discarding of a wonted point of view in favor of a radical alternative. It is not a matter of seeing more deeply what is initially perceived dimly or inchoately. It is a matter of seeing differently, of substituting and replacing insights instead of adding to them. The calculated absurdity of O'Connor's rendering, the detachment fostered by comic treatment, and the lack of explanations effectively inhibit sympathy or imaginative identification with fictional personality and predicament.

On the basis of these observations, it seems reasonable to conclude that the effects of O'Connor's use of the grotesque are sometimes not the ones that she anticipated. To experience what O'Connor apparently desired her stories to communicate, one not only would have to identify with her fictional representation of life, but further, would have to infer the cause of broken absurdities in both fiction and self to be the lack of God. In the cases at hand, the sto-

ries evoke both uneasy laughter and tension. But to say that the ugliness recognizable in them also elicits a sense of theological "mystery" is unwarranted; for in the contexts that O'Connor has created,
deformity is ultimately ambiguous in origin. At this point, it is germane to inquire whether O'Connor used the rhetorical strategies of
the realistic tradition with a greater certainty of effect.

FOUR

The Rhetorical Uses of Analogy and Allusion

The eye sees what it has been given to see by concrete circumstances.

[The writer's] problem is really how to make the concrete work double time for him.

Flannery O'Connor
Mystery and Manners

I

Using *realism* as a descriptive term for O'Connor's fiction is problematic on several accounts. The most obvious reason is that the convention is inseparable from the commitment to represent the concrete world with fidelity—a commitment that O'Connor violated frequently. Beyond this obvious deviation from tradition, there is a further problem with O'Connor's work that can be stated initially as a semantic dilemma: the artist did not think that reality was Reality.

I take this discrimination to be O'Connor's reformulation of the common opposition between appearance and reality, with this distinction: for her, reality was not the tangible world encountered without delusion, but a dimension of perception perhaps fostered by, but ultimately transcending, the substantial field of sense impressions. Whereas appearances are given, reality is constructed, or, as O'Connor put it, it must be "returned to"; and she was anxious that her readers return to it according to a preconceived, revealed body of meaning.[1] The key word is *revealed*, for the final authority for knowledge of this sort is not the experience of the senses, but the word of God, in whatever form that may take—scripture or personal vision.

As long as we have no reason to doubt it, appearance is simply the aspect under which reality is presented to us. Only when given circumstances are incompatible with each other does a distinction between deceptive and nondeceptive aspects of experience need to be made, and only then does the concept of reality become dissociated from appearance. Similarly in fiction, an incongruity of narrative events signals that we are to mistrust appearances, which, in themselves, do not lead to the truth. On a very simple level, this disjunction occurs with what we normally call dramatic irony—a reader or viewer recognizing that a character makes an incorrect or partial assessment of his circumstances. For example, Mrs. Turpin, in O'Connor's story "Revelation," considers her main asset to be a good disposition, but her actions and conversation show her to be, in fact, offensively complacent and bigoted. But O'Connor is normally straining beyond this simple fictional situation, working not with two appearances that are discrepant (for example, a remark that belies a self-image) but with an incongruity between the concrete reality in her stories and a radically different spiritual order standing behind it.

The intention to indicate that there is an antagonism between sensory appearance and meaning, that the world of appearances in some way obscures a transcendent reality, fosters a paradoxical situation in which the concrete terms of the narrative must be set up to be discredited. That is, the author must indicate that the world of sense impressions is ultimately either untrustworthy or simply incomplete; she must intimate that there is something more to be noticed than what is rendered.

This is a difficult problem, for as Yvor Winters points out, this world, though it may be in ultimate terms an illusion, is precisely the world in which we act and perceive and make moral decisions; and of more direct importance here, it is the embodiment of this area of experience that engenders the Jamesian sense of "felt life" in fiction.[2] In fact, it is the acuteness of rendering on this realistic level that courts a reader's assent to the text. O'Connor was quick to realize this. "I think the more a writer wishes to make the supernatural apparent, the more real he has to be able to make the natural world, for if the readers don't accept the natural world, they'll certainly not accept anything else."[3] Her way "out" was couched in somewhat enigmatic terms and, in one instance, in the language of theology; the writer of extended and mystical vision should intimate the invisible dimension of his personal reality by making "the concrete work double time for him," by effecting an "incarnational art."[4]

To speak of spirit incarnate in matter is to address the specifically Christian mystery of transubstantiation, the situation in which a thing can be itself and at the same time something else. The best example of this is the Eucharist, the fusion of Christ's blood and wine, of His body and a wafer. But in a more expanded sense, this notion of transubstantiation is at the base of the literary understanding of a symbol as well. For one speaks of a symbol in both poetry and prose as having a similar mystery, of retaining a concrete and specific identity while concurrently standing for something more abstract.[5] It was probably in this sense that O'Connor identified her narrative as "incarnational" or as working double time, even though she was publicly dubious about using symbols (note her widely quoted remark about the Eucharist: "If it were only a symbol, I'd say to hell with it").[6] This metamorphic imaginative habit may have led a number of her critics to identify her with the school of nineteenth-century American romanticism and to see in her work the same transcendental tendency to regard nature as a shorthand for corresponding moral significances.[7]

But placing O'Connor's writing in the tradition of religious incarnation or transcendental correspondence can create a major interpretive dilemma. The danger arises precisely out of the cultural situation that obsessed and enraged O'Connor: society no longer derives a collective perspective from Christian myth. The problem is clarified if we distinguish between two kinds of symbols in literature. There is what Mary McCarthy calls "the natural symbolism of reality," by which she refers to the significance accorded to fictional events, the importance of the incidents themselves, as drawn from reflection on those incidents. And there is a more contrived symbol, whereby a fictional object is intended to relate to a system of meaning that exists beyond and apart from the story.[8] It is the latter situation that O'Connor wanted to effect in her narratives: to designate the concrete circumstance and to point with it toward a theological system of values. However, it is specifically this kind of symbolism that is unviable in an agnostic literary milieu, since a readership untutored in religious symbolism will not know to attach a spiritual significance to, for example, the sun, though it may see very clearly that the author intends the sun to be important.

Although the suggestion may seem radical, "the spirit incarnate in matter" is not in itself a dramatizable concept, because a reader does not know what system of meaning, exterior to the text, to associate with an *unadorned* natural event, even though he may sense, through repetition or patterning, that an object is indeed intended to demonstrate something more than meets the eye. "In this dream forest," McCarthy wrote, "symbols become arbitrary; all counters are interchangeable; anything can stand for anything else. The Colonel's hash [referring to her own story 'Artists in Uniform'] can be a Eucharist or a cannibal feast or the banquet of Atreus."[9] She has stated here, in farfetched terms, the problem anticipated by Herman Melville in the nineteenth century, that we no longer know how to interpret coherently the signs that the phenomenal world puts forth; nor do we, by extension, have the assurance that the concrete signifies anything universal at all. As Melville recognized, the "pasteboard masks" may have nothing behind them that our fancies have not put there. O'Connor saw this modern impulse, was repulsed by it, and mocked contemporary men as having "no country broader than the sides of their skulls."[10] But as much as she may have hated the solipsism and relativity of the current social situation, it remains a cultural phenomenon that will not disappear by disparaging it.

Melville, it must be pointed out, found an alternative method to ensure unambiguous interpretation of symbols. He rendered both term and referent in the text. A famous but pointed example in *Moby Dick* is Ishmael's Loom of Time meditation, in which the action of weaving illustrates, by prolonged image, the interrelations of a difficult philosophical problem:

> There lay the fixed threads of the warp subject to but one single, ever returning, unchanging vibration, and that vibration merely enough to admit of the crosswise interblending of other threads with its own. This warp seemed necessity; and here, thought I, with my own hand I ply my own shuttle and weave my own destiny into these unalterable threads. Meantime, Queequeg's impulsive, indifferent sword, sometimes hitting the woof slantingly, or crookedly, or strongly, or weakly, as the case might be; and by this difference in the concluding blow producing a corresponding contrast in the final aspect of the completed fabric; this savage's sword, thought I, which thus finally shapes and fashions both warp and woof; this easy, indifferent sword must be chance—ay, chance, free will, and necessity—no wise incompatible—all interweavingly working together. The straight warp of necessity, not to be swerved from its ultimate course—its every alternating vibration, indeed, only tending to that; free will still free to ply her shuttle between given threads; and chance, though restrained in its play within the right lines of necessity, and sideways in its motions directed by free will, though thus prescribed to by both, chance by turns rules either, and has the last featuring blow at events.[11]

As F. O. Matthiessen observes about the passage, the details have been subordinated to their application and the "point by point correspondence establishes the interworking of 'chance, free will, and necessity' with a clarity more decisive than pages of argument."[12] It should be emphasized that, even though the abstractions illustrated by the physical structure have been brought explicitly to the surface, Melville never abandons the nautical source of his speculation. The narrative and its interpretation are equally accessible, and since Melville's commitment to finding significance in natural phenomena finds expression on the literal level of exposition, there is no need for a reader to deduce another ulterior meaning.

Besides the method of direct meditation, the dramatized speculation about the meanings of particular areas of experience, the writer of transcendental concerns also has the use of analogy as a technical resource. In this case, it is particularly valuable because it enables a reader to formulate an hypothesis for verification by induction. The concrete terms of the analogy (*phoroi*), can serve as a premise for inferring, through resemblance of structures, what cannot be known directly (a theme). In O'Connor's writing the concrete language of analogy does have a dual function. Indeed, this is one of the commonest teaching devices of philosophy and religion, as this example from Plotinus indicates. "As spoken language is but a splintering of words compared to the inward language of the soul, so the language of the soul which interprets the divine Word is but a fragment when it is compared to the Word."[13] In other cases an analogy can be condensed, that is, two of its four terms (a:b::c:d) can be submerged, and one recognizes the resultant construction as a metaphor. This device is the basis for many of Christ's parables ("For the Kingdom of Heaven is like to a grain of mustard seed" [Matthew 13:31]); for the descriptions of the spiritual kingdom in the Christian apocalyptic literature ("And the building of the wall of it was of jasper and the city was pure gold, like unto clear glass" [Revelation 21:18]); and the Zen story about the nature of Buddha, who is said to be variously "the blossoming branch of a plum tree," "a pink fish with golden fins swimming idly through the blue sea," and "the full moon cold and silent in the night sky, turning the dark meadow to silver."[14]

Such metaphor is not merely an ornamental image offering vividness or color; rather it serves, along with more extended analogy, as a basis for inference, for expecting that the theme (in these instances taken from the spiritual realm) will have a likeness to what can be observed. And occasionally a single *phoros* will be inadequate to explain the intended theme, but several *phoroi* can be used to impress a general direction of thought. Cervantes described Don Quixote in this way: "For a knight errant without a lady is like a tree without leaves, a building without mortar, or a shadow without a body that causes it." [15] He desired to emphasize more than a single image could suggest about the barren, aimless quality of a life without coherent purpose.

O'Connor's analogical impulse was an early and pervasive habit. She used it in various and unorthodox ways and with effects that are much more readily accessible than any symbolic attempts to load nature with the weight of the transcendent world. Take, for example, these descriptions: "The foot was in a heavy black battered shoe with a sole four or five inches thick. The leather parted from it in one place and the end of an empty sock protruded like a grey tongue from a severed head"; "They walked to the river, Mrs. Connin in front with him and the three boys strung out behind. . . . They looked like the skeleton of an old boat with two pointed ends"; and "Her eyes were as hard as two old mountain ranges seen in the distance." [16] In these and many similar comparisons, both the implicit ones of metaphor and the explicit ones of simile, the *phoroi*, that is, the second terms of the comparison, are often chosen to be extraordinarily startling; the juxtaposition of terms is intended to shock and disquiet in the interest of forcing judgment or manipulating sympathies. Used in this normative way, these jarring comparisons serve as an aspect of the grotesque, as part of a larger strategy to dehumanize and distance the human life rendered.

Along with this tendency to parody and estrange by improbable juxtapositions, O'Connor used analogies for comedy, for intensified dramatic effect, and, one can hypothesize, to make essential connections between the material world and its "revealed" meaning as her own beliefs dictated that meaning. The following section will focus on a few of the stories that have pronounced metaphoric emphasis, but first a few relevant questions should be isolated.

Returning briefly to the example of Melville, it is possible to see that author's struggle to understand the various moral significances of the natural world fully dramatized in the fiction as Ishmael's dilemma. When the central character is not able to narrate, the voice of the author assumes the speculation so that the problem of correspondences, of seeing and understanding the import of natural events, is consistently before the reader. By contrast, O'Connor's assumptions about spirit in matter are rarely the topic of exposition.[17] The absence of explicit comment about the problems of assigning extended meaning to physical events forces the reader to consider such extensions of meaning only through inference, as he sifts out the importance of juxtapositions—Negroes and nut grass, hands and lilies, a car and an arc, clouds and white fish. Further, there is no working out of point-by-point correspondences so that a certain interpretation will be inevitable.

One can speculate that O'Connor's romantic tendency to analogize was kept in check by a self-conscious discipline which had its origins in the Jamesian belief that the dramatic force of short story writing would be dissipated by interpretive reflection. Regardless of the source of this reticence, the analogies in the stories and novels are rarely elaborated. They appear repeatedly, with apparent intention, but with a sporadic recurrence that is finally problematic. Are these allusions incidental and specific? That is, is their embellishment intended to bring isolated moments of pictorial intensity, or do they form parts of more extended, though indirect and fragmented, motifs? Finally, assuming that such themes can be located, when do their meanings overtake and obscure the literal events of the story, demanding what is, in essence, an allegorical "playing out" of the literal events on a second, abstract level of understanding?

II

The narrative pattern of O'Connor's story "Greenleaf" is one that has by now become familiar: unexpected violence forces a farm widow to reevaluate her life. Although Mrs. May's death is a freak accident—a bull rams into her as she leans against a truck fender—it is clear that dying effects a change in her perspective. O'Connor tells us at the moment of disaster and before Mrs. May slumps in death that "she had the look of a person whose sight has been suddenly restored but who finds the light unbearable." [18] And her appearance to the hired hand who runs to help her is that of a person "bent over whispering some last discovery into the animal's ear" (334). In consequence of these descriptions, the import of this event is unambiguously connected with a revelation; but we have known since Mrs. May muttered to her sons, "You'll find out one of these days, you'll find out what Reality is when it's too late!" (320) that how to evaluate reality has been a perennial issue with these cantankerous people. The problem is not simply to identify the moment of insight, but to ascribe a more specific content to Mrs. May's final vision. What particular version of reality has this woman seen, ironically, when "it's too late?"

One way of coming to terms with this question is to assign special significance to the bull that gores Mrs. May, that is, to discover, through metaphor and allusion, secondary levels of implication in the actions of the farm animal. In terms of the plot, this critical attention is warranted, for the bull is so extraordinarily important to Mrs. May that she spends all her time trying to capture him.

In identifying the motivations for this character's obsession, in coming to understand the particular meaning that the Greenleaf bull has for her, a reader discovers Mary McCarthy's "natural symbolism." He pieces together the significance that the animal has for Mrs. May, and by this process of reflection, comes to see the complexity and submerged implications inherent in natural events.

To understand how this happens, the circumstances of the bull's escapades should be examined. He escapes from his pen on the property of some "hired help" and arrives during the night at the farm of the brittle, highly agitated widow, Mrs. May. The story, a pastiche of narrative in the present, memory, and private reflections on "typical" behavior ("Mr. Greenleaf would say that"), shows Mrs. May to be a woman who works feverishly to contain her paranoia.

The remark, "I'm the victim. I've always been the victim" (327), discloses her perception of personal circumstances, and this sense of persecution focuses on the Greenleaf family. It is not difficult to surmise the reason, for the story sets up an explicit comparison between Mrs. May's two sons and those of her farm hand, Mr. Greenleaf. The latter boys have traveled in Europe, married foreign wives, been educated as part of a GI bill, and purchased efficient farm machinery through the government. By contrast, using Mrs. May's own standards of evaluation, her own boys are negligible—one a sour intellectual and the other a "policy man" for Negroes. This situation of older generations taking their pride and sense of accomplishment largely from the achievements of their children occasions the covert antagonism between Mr. Greenleaf and Mrs. May ("My boys done it ... but all boys ain't alike" [324]) and causes Mrs. May to goad her own lunking children into more active, "decent" lives. It is also the humiliated frustration of having lazy, ill-disposed sons that prompts her remark "You'll find out what Reality is when it's too late."

The background of the bull's visit is, then, a highly charged life circumstance in which a woman tries to maintain a sense of self-respect in front of her hired help, while privately holding up the same help's boys as models for her own sons. What is at stake is both the viability of Mrs. May's value system, a narrow work ethic that is openly defied by Wesley and Scofield May, and defeat by the standards that such a system offers. Mrs. May is afraid of white "trash" surpassing her social status through their own industry. This sense of victimization, the feeling of self-pity occasioned by profligate offspring, extends beyond her conflict with the Greenleafs ("'Everything is against you,' she would say, 'the weather is against you and the dirt is against you and the help is against you'" [321]), but it is centered on it.

So it is not surprising that the escaped bull should be more than a usual irritant to Mrs. May. He is, after all, a Greenleaf bull, and she attributes conscious malice to his presence on her lawn. The following passage describes her first sleepy premonition of him.

> She had been conscious in her sleep of a steady rhyth-
> mic chewing as if something were eating one wall of
> the house. She had been aware that whatever it was
> had been eating as long as she had had the place and
> had eaten everything from the beginning of her fence
> line up to the house and now was eating the house and
> calmly with the same steady rhythm would continue
> through the house, eating her and the boys, and then
> on, eating everything but the Greenleafs, on and on,
> eating everything until nothing was left but the Green-
> leafs on a little island all their own in the middle of
> what had been her place. When the munching reached
> her elbow, she jumped up and found herself, fully
> awake, standing in the middle of her room. She identi-
> fied the sound at once: a cow was tearing at the shrub-
> bery under her window. Mr. Greenleaf had left the land
> gate open and she didn't doubt that the entire herd was
> on her lawn. She turned on the dim pink table lamp
> and then went to the window and slit the blind. The
> bull, gaunt and long-legged, was standing about four
> feet from her, chewing calmly like an uncouth country
> suitor. (311–12)

The prose is remarkable on several accounts. For one thing, the par-
agraph begins with a conjectural comparison: the chewing sounds
as if the frame of the house is being consumed. The conditional
form of the phrase is important, for what is literally untrue nonetheless carries a pointed psychological validity; the analogy allows the
author to render a subjective impression with the weight of objective reality. And indeed, in the course of relating this impression,
the voice changes to the indicative mode, narrating what is so
highly improbable ("when the munching reached her elbow, she")
that the interpretation is forced from a literal to the figurative plane.
Considered in this light, it is the impression that is important, the
motion of the perceiving consciousness; and, in particular, it is the
paranoia or fear of life impinging on and consuming the self that
impresses the reader. In short, the bull acts as a catalyst for Mrs.

May's most deep-seated anxieties; he activates the woman's fear of defeat by some force that will destroy everything *except* the Green-leafs. It is not, then, a generalized phobia, but a fear that arises out of Mrs. May's tendency to see life in terms of conflict between family and family. As such, the conjectural description contributes to our understanding of the central opposition in this brief tale and to our seeing that the stakes of the confrontation are survival itself. Then, at the end of this passage, O'Connor adds a remarkable simile: the bull chews calmly in the garden, "like an uncouth country suitor."

The density and complexity of passages like this can be accounted for partly by the narrator's chameleon voice. For the metaphor that concludes the description of subjective point of view in no way reflects that limited perspective. Mrs. May is exceedingly irritated at the bull; she does not regard him in any way as a suitor. Given this incongruity, the only possible conclusion is that the narrative voice has shifted and makes the analogy in address to the reader. In fact, the voice has apparently resumed the omniscience that marked the story's opening when the bull was described, again by analogy, as a "patient god come down to woo her" (311). These embellishments continue with the conjecture that some hedge greenery is like a "wreath across his [the bull's] horns" and, further, that this wreath is like "a menacing prickly crown" (312).

What are we to make of these analogies? Mary McCarthy once remarked that "a book is not a pious excuse for reciting a litany of associations," and she was quite right.[19] But O'Connor's impulse to compare is insistent, and it is safe to assume that these metaphors, these deliberate attempts to expand the semantic field of the word *bull* by association, are headed somewhere.

Usually they have been assumed to head toward the Bible. An example of this interpretive tendency is found in this comment: "Symbolically the bull first appears as a god . . . to the Christian, this imagery (the wreath) suggests the God-man, Christ, at the hour of his passion and death." By extending this allusion, the commentator reads the narrative as Mrs. May's "encounter with the divine" and concludes that the final encounter (the death by goring) is the experience of grace. The moral follows quickly: "The measure of a man's openness to . . . grace is the measure of his truthful perception of reality." [20] Another critic begins with the question "How do you make the goring of a woman by a bull a spiritual event?" But he has already made the assumption that this event is not only spiritual but spiritual in a specifically theological sense. "In the process by which the bull comes to symbolize something more mysterious than a dumb beast, one can see the operation of O'Connor's aesthetic habit of endowing the flesh with a spiritual significance; while in the agony of the woman's death, one can see an accession to mystery through the painful annihilation of the flesh." [21]

In the first instance, the commentator begins with an interpretation that follows for a specialized group—the Christians. But it should be reemphasized that O'Connor did not write primarily for believers, but for "lost" souls, for her "monstrous readers." The critic uses the wrong model for the reader and, in consequence, derives a textual meaning that is not necessarily accessible to an agnostic. In the second case, the critic resorts to the mystical vocabulary of "the flesh [endowed] with spiritual significance." However, the Greenleaf bull is not just a symbol, but a farm animal with a complicated but identifiable set of associations. He has not metamorphized into something unsubstantial, and he is not consequently the key to an allegorical reading of the text. The aesthetic process by which he assumes added significance deserves more careful scrutiny than the language of mystic transformation provides.

When we consider the associations that embellish O'Connor's description of the bull, their density is immediately apparent. The beast is variously an awkward lover, a patient god, and the bearer of an unorthodox wreath. Thus there are sexual associations, intimations of classical divinity (Jupiter, the bull as disguised god-lover) and of the Christian passion (Jesus' crown of thorns at the time of his persecution). The textual situation is one in which multiple *phoroi* are used by the author to explain a single theme, and the multiplicity of references has independent conceptual implications. Far from calling for a selection of one comparative term (for example, the Christian one), the complexity of the narrative suggests that cumulative definition is necessary, that each *phoros* taken separately is inadequate to the author's purpose. Given this narrative circumstance, a reader sifts through the comparative terms that are offered to discover the general direction of thought that they collectively extend. In this case, the analogies occur in the context of a woman's paranoia; they fit into a larger pattern of rendering the pursuer and the pursued. It does not seem to matter, then, whether the bull is a suffering Christ, a Roman divinity, or a country lover, for these terms commonly contribute a sense of life forces that impinge on and threaten a mind closely programmed to exclude the irrational.

Other similar narrative descriptions reinforce this sense of Mrs. May's fear. The sun is rendered with the same subjective bias that characterized the bull's presentation. For example, after Mrs. May had peered into the spotless Greenleaf dairy, she closed the door and "was conscious that the sun was directly on top of her head like a silver bullet ready to drop into her brain" (325). Later, in a dream, "she became aware after a time that the noise was the sun trying to burn through the tree line and she stopped to watch, safe in the knowledge that it couldn't, that it had to sink the way it always did outside of her property. When she first stopped it was a swollen red ball, but as she stood watching it began to narrow and pale until it looked like a bullet. Then suddenly it burst through the tree line and raced down the hill toward her" (329). If we take the sun as an instance of metonymy, of a part representing the whole, these passages offer a further image of the woman's obsession with her own impotent position in a hostile universe. That she is pursued by something she cannot control is consistent with her attitude toward religion, for her objection to Mrs. Greenleaf's prayer healing, for example, is primarily a reaction to its lack of containment. One day, the narrative recounts, she found her neighbor prone in the dirt, "a huge human mound, her legs and arms spread out as if she were trying to wrap them around the earth" (317). The woman's sprawl and her guttural, "terrible" groaning "Jesus! Jesus!" are obviously sexual. That Mrs. May makes this association is evidenced in the comment, "She thought the word, Jesus, should be kept inside the church building like other words inside the bedroom" (317). But again, the linking of religion and sex, the multiple allusion, identifies the problem as greater than either referent. Together they help to identify a fear of something no more specific than a "violent, unleashed force," a fear of the irrational.

The end of the Greenleaf story dramatizes, in effect, the protagonist's encounter with what represents her fears. In a final sense, Mrs. May is the victim of irrational force, overcome by it even as she fantasizes about subduing her antagonist, whom she still perceives to be the Greenleaf family. Her fantasy of the bull killing the hired man is essentially a dream of herself triumphant over all that the Greenleafs represent to her, and the irony is, of course, apparent. It is Mrs. May who succumbs.

The parallel circumstance of Mrs. May's death and Mrs. Greenleaf's plea ("Jesus stab me in the heart!") has sometimes been used to support the interpretation that the bull is Jesus and, consequently, that the goring enacts the woman's encounter with God. It is impossible to ignore this parallelism, this twisted analogy of incident; but to elevate it to an inclusive explanation of the text is, I feel, to give final authority to what is incidental in effect. The threat posed by the Greenleafs, by recalcitrant children, by the desperate position of solitude in an indifferent and troublesome environment, is a complex problem, and it engenders a complex response. As ridiculous and narrow as Mrs. May may seem in her attempts to contain these menacing aspects of her life, her difficult circumstances are occasioned by more than a misplaced attitude toward religion. The natural allusions, sexual innuendos, and economic and social issues posed collectively ensure that this prose is read in dense and subtle ways. Furthermore, calling the bull an agent of destruction and the catalyst for Mrs. May's awakening is totally different from contending that the bull is an example of spirit incarnate in flesh, a symbol of grace. Revelation of supreme and final human vulnerability is not solely a lesson of Christian theology, but the insight of anyone capable of seeing beyond Mrs. May's narrow ethic of making gardens and washing clothes; and certainly the time for such altered perspective is at the point of death.

III

In the introduction to this chapter it was pointed out that analogy or metaphor can be used to indicate the nature of spiritual reality—a dimension of life that is not directly accessible to the senses but that can be inferred by an implied similarity of structures. In each example given to illustrate the process, the theme was taken from the spiritual realm and identified by a concrete *phoros*: Buddha is like, heaven is like, the Word of God is like. The intelligence is directed to the unknown by means of what is known. But minimal consideration of O'Connor's stories reveals that the author's analogies begin with the concrete world as theme, and the process of inference leads us not directly to spirit, but to an expanded sense of the physical environment. This is certainly true of the Greenleaf bull; what we know of this class of farm animal is manipulated and enlarged with reference to myths or attributes not usually associated with bulls, but that are also knowable in themselves. The known is compared to the known, and extra meaning accrues from selecting points of similarity in unusually juxtaposed items. Such emphasis on comparison places the process of deciphering O'Connor's fiction within the realm of understandable intelligence; it demystifies the prose and moves the discussion of fiction away from parareligious critical language like "the transformation of naturalistic surface into theological mystery."[22] This is especially important when we realize that many of O'Connor's allusions (which act, after all, as the *phoroi* in an analogical process of understanding) are not to mystery in the abstract, but to Christian myths, to the substance of Christ's life. These stories contain facts that are accessible to even the most agnostic reader in the same way that allusion to classical mythology can be identified. As Northrop Frye has said, "The literary critic, like the historian, is compelled to treat every religion in the same way that religions treat each other, as though it were a human hypothesis, whatever else he may in other contexts believe it to be."[23]

When such references occur, the critic must determine the extent of their application, for a distinction must be made between the incidental and specific mythical allusion and a parallelism of fictional circumstances that occasions fitting the total narrative into the structure of myth. Several major critical studies of O'Connor's work have suggested structural parallelism where none is legitimately deducible.[24] It is with the intention of clarifying the limits of allusive references that we turn now to a reading of "The Displaced Person."

The story of the displaced person is, as we have come to expect of O'Connor, a narrative about the radical disruption of commonplace life. Unlike the violent experiences of loss in "Good Country People" and "A Circle in the Fire," the incidents that interrupt the routine of the McIntyre farm occur gradually, with the result that the implications of clashing value systems are developed with more subtlety or nuance than is common in O'Connor's short fiction.

At the instigation of a local priest, the widow, Mrs. McIntyre, agrees to hire a Polish war refugee to help on her farm. The foreign man's arrival with his family is a critical event to both the Negroes and the other farmhands, but Mr. Guizac's presence especially disturbs a hired man's wife. In part one of the story, the nature and consequences of this threat are revealed; in parts two and three, the Pole's behavior alienates Mrs. McIntyre. There are, then, two separate confrontations, between Mr. Guizac and Mrs. Shortley, and Mr. Guizac and Mrs. McIntyre; and throughout the encounters, the priest bobs in and out making low-key inquiries and feeding a lone peacock.

In a certain way, it is misleading to represent these fictional events as encounters, for nothing so formal happens. The narrative moves between "a plain old story" told from an omniscient vantage point and the rendering of subjective points of view. Mr. Guizac is known primarily as he impresses first Mrs. Shortley, then Mrs. McIn-

tyre. Thus the story is in effect an account of developing consciousness in relation to a European refugee, and the process by
which O'Connor establishes the special meaning of the Pole's conduct to each woman is centrally important.

To Mrs. Shortley, the Guizacs are initially disturbing because she
associates them with the holocaust of World War II. In a series of
metaphors designed to disclose Mrs. Shortley's perspective rather
than offer an objective evaluation, the mother of the family is described as a peanut, the daughter as a bug, and collectively they are
said to be like "rats with typhoid fleas." These images arise from fear
of the alien, from a distrust of what cannot be understood, though
the images are constructed from the prejudices of the mass media,
not from face-to-face judgment. In fact, after Mrs. Shortley has privately rehearsed her image of Europeans as either jumbled together
in a mass of broken limbs or walking single file in Dutchmen's
shoes, it is difficult for her to adjust to the evidence of her senses:
these people look like anyone else. Not wholly the product of a
morbid and misinformed imagination, this woman's sense of danger
also arises from evaluation of a realistic situation: the Polish man is a
model of industry and technical expertise, whereas her own husband is a slipshod, careless worker. In time, the contrast in caliber is
so apparent that the Shortleys know they will be asked to leave. In
their hasty, distraught exodus, Mrs. Shortley has a frenetic vision
and dies. The daughters are unable to grasp the situation. "They
didn't know that she had had a great experience or ever been displaced in the world from all that belonged to her."[25] However
much the daughters may miss in the experience, a reader cannot
overlook the analogy between Mrs. Shortley's concept of European
refugees as a pile of disassembled bodies, and the context of her
own upset, reaching as she does in the overcrowded car for Mr.
Shortley's head, Sarah Mae's leg, and "her own big moon-like knee."
Quite clearly O'Connor has created an inversion, an intended play
on the reversed circumstances of foreigner and native, but we are
never told what the substance of Mrs. Shortley's vision is. If we are
really to infer that her "true country" is death, then the central dis-

placement is that experience of death, and not the temporal up-
rooting occasioned by Mr. Guizac's employment.

In contrast, Mrs. McIntyre's reaction to the Pole is initially one of
great satisfaction. Far from being threatened, she is delighted by
Guizac's industry and values the man in proportion to the money
he saves her. He is "a kind of miracle" that is "not very real to her
yet" (219). This delight continues until Guizac's private concern to
bring a young European cousin to America by marrying her to one
of the black workers shakes Mrs. McIntyre's entire opinion of him.
The value of his industry is obscured at this point by his "foreign"
social behavior. Mrs. McIntyre envisions the effects of this intention, not in terms of saving the young girl from the ghetto, but according to the disruption to farm life that an interracial marriage
would occasion. In response to the offense she feels at Guizac's un-
acceptable ideas, Mrs. McIntyre resolves to dismiss him, but she
procrastinates until an accident is "allowed" to happen. The Pole is
crushed under a tractor in front of Mr. Shortley, Mrs. McIntyre, and
Sulk, whose eyes come together "in one look that froze them in col-
lusion forever" (234). As the last rites are administered by the
priest, Mrs. McIntyre experiences the same sense of displacement
that had supposedly characterized Mrs. Shortley's last moments.
The question of foreigner and native is raised once again with a similar implication of inversion, so that Mrs. McIntyre, like her estate
manageress, is seen to be a stranger to a particular area of experience. In another parallel and ironic circumstance, all the farm
hands leave Mrs. McIntyre's farm, thereby extending the question
of who is, this time physically, displaced in the world.

Robert Fitzgerald has said of this story that it constitutes the
"classic situation of tragedy in which each party to the conflict is
both right and wrong and almost incomprehensible to the other." [26]
Clearly the difficulties between the two women and Guizac represent a confrontation of value systems, one deriving from the prejudices and social situation of the South, the other an outgrowth of
suffering and an extremity of experience unimaginable to the parochial American women. Need we go any farther into the story

to see that displacement occurs when operative values are radically challenged, to see the tenuous grounds of our temporal society? To some extent, the answer lies in our attitude toward the Polish man Guizac who, like the Greenleaf bull, is a catalyst for altered consciousness.

What of this little bespectacled man? He is industrious, perhaps from habit, but certainly out of necessity. He is honest in a social situation where dishonesty is an institutionalized part of racial and class relationships, and he is a complete outsider in a culture untempered by modern war and in a land supremely conscious of protocol in race relations. However, Guizac is also an outsider to the reader, for he is described only as he is seen externally; the narrator never claims access to his mind. Even at this distance, he is never described with the halo of metaphor that surrounded the Greenleaf bull. At one time he is said to be like a monkey; elsewhere he is designated as a financial miracle. But these overt similes are scant, unpatterned, and thus ornamental. The association of Guizac with a wider range of significance is accomplished by another means, by what is, in fact, a deliberately executed semantic confusion. In conversation, Mrs. McIntyre tries to tell the priest why she is not responsible for the plight of Mr. Guizac. The priest, who is watching a peacock unfurl his splendid tail, remarks of the bird, "Christ will come like that! . . . the transfiguration!" Mrs. McIntyre pursues her original line of thought with "He didn't have to come here in the first place," to which the priest responds absently and according to his own preoccupation, "He came to redeem us" (226). The ambiguity of pronoun references to Guizac and Christ is impossible to miss; and it is intended for the reader, since neither speaker in the fictional situation realizes what the other individual has said; they have responded according to private obsessions. The deliberate artifice is reconfirmed in a later conversation when Mrs. McIntyre dismisses the priest's evangelizing with, "As far as I'm concerned . . . Christ was just another D.P." (229).

Thus there is in the fiction a purposeful association of the contemporary refugee with the central character of Christian myth. It is known that in Mrs. McIntyre's mind, Christ and the displaced person have something in common, and by virtue of the previously noted ambiguity, it can be surmised that this is not intended to remain solely as the revelation of limited point of view. It has the full sanction of the narrating voice. However, it is appropriate to ask whether this association constitutes grounds for concluding that Guizac represents Christ and that his death is a reenactment of Christ's passion. To make this assumption (and it has frequently been made) is to confuse a specific reference to a myth in a story that takes its shape from a contemporary situation, with another kind of story whose narrative pattern is made to accord with the whole action of a myth. As previously shown, there is a distinction between an author's reference to myth and mythic narrative structure, and this is precisely the place to apply that discrimination. The reference to Christ occurs in the context of a complex social and psychological dilemma. To isolate the Christ analogy and elevate it to the status of the story's meaning is to ignore the realistic racial, social, and personal difficulties that create the story's texture and whose implications are at the heart of its meaning. Even if we ignore the critical poverty of eliciting abstract meaning from a text as if it were a thread in a chicken feed sack, this elevation of Christian myth to a central interpretive position changes the plane on which the fiction is received from realism to myth.[27] It refuses to read the account of human dilemma as human dilemma rather than divine encounter.[28] Denying the analogy of Christ's and Guizac's experience of rejection is senseless, because the reference is blatant; but accrediting this allusion, giving it the proper interpretive weight is central to the critic's task. In this instance, the reference adds to, but is subsidiary to, the realistic surface of the text. Insofar as Guizac and Christ have been resented for suggesting alternative and unpragmatic value systems, their lives have a common aspect. But this does not make O'Connor's alienated Pole a symbol for God incarnate. At most and, in my opinion, with greatest effect, the analogy places the experience charted on Mrs. McIntyre's farm in the context of an archetypal situation of human intolerance. It tells us gently that this has happened before.

I extend this reading even though O'Connor would have been disappointed with it. She consistently resisted interpretations that "leveled" her writing to its social, psychological, and economic components. To her, they were the work of people with limited insight, of a piece with the review of *A Good Man is Hard to Find* in which "The Displaced Person" first appeared. "The notice in *The New Yorker* was not only moronic, it was unsigned. It was a case in which it is easy to see that the moral sense has been bred out of certain sections of the population, like the wings have been bred off certain chickens to produce more white meat on them." But to her credit, she did not rest with shifting blame, and this was one story that continued to disquiet her. "The displaced person did accomplish a kind of redemption in that he destroyed the place, which was evil, and set Mrs. McIntyre on the road to a new kind of suffering. . . . None of this was adequately shown and to make the story complete it would have had to be—so I did fail myself. Understatement was not enough . . . but how are you going to make such things clear to people who don't believe in God, much less in Purgatory?"[29] The problem of audience was clearly still with her.

In the two stories discussed here, analogy and allusion contribute to an expanded sense of meaning in the texts, but they do so only by using themes and *phoroi* that are both identifiable. Analogy, for example, does not function, as it often does in religious teaching, to direct the intelligence toward a transcendent unknown. Instead, the expansion is worked by comparing something that is known to something else that is also known. Although analogy may use Christian myth as one of its referents, the comparison does not serve as a key to revealed truth. Its status is exactly the same as any other reference, be it psychology or classicism. At most, it tells us what Caroline Gordon has said elsewhere: O'Connor had no classical education and thus had only her theological training as a source of narrative embellishment.[30] In all cases, however, allusion and analogy function in a subsidiary way. They enrich the texture of realistic narration without usurping the realistic surface with abstract, revealed meanings.

As will become more apparent, O'Connor's writing is heavily allusive, and in her last novel, *The Violent Bear It Away*, she used biblical references to create one entire side of the central narrative conflict: young Tarwater's debate about the relative merits of the "bread of life" and material well being. In this novel, the allusions are clear; but once the references are identified, questions still remain. Is the metaphysical "hunger" shown to be better than literal hunger; is madness shown to be a higher order of wisdom than traditional values? The next rhetorical strategy to be examined is the way in which the author defines the precise ordering of values on which a reader's judgment depends, even when biblical references are clearly presented.

FIVE

Control of Distance
in *The Violent Bear It*
Away

He stood there, straining forward, but the scene faded
in the gathering darkness. Night descended until there
was nothing but a thin streak of red between it and the
black line of earth but still he stood there. He felt his
hunger no longer as a pain but as a tide. He felt it rising
in himself through time and darkness, rising through
the centuries, and he knew that it rose in a line of men
whose lives were chosen to sustain it, who would
wander in the world, strangers from that violent country where the silence is never broken except to shout
the truth. He felt it building from the blood of Abel to
his own, rising and engulfing him. It seemed in one instant to lift and turn him. He whirled toward the treeline. There, rising and spreading in the night, a red-gold
tree of fire ascended as if it would consume the darkness in one tremendous burst of flame. The boy's
breath went out to meet it. He knew that this was the
fire that had encircled Daniel, that had raised Elijah
from the earth, that had spoken to Moses and would in
the instant speak to him. He threw himself to the
ground and with his face against the dirt of the grave,
he heard the command. GO WARN THE CHILDREN OF

GOD OF THE TERRIBLE SPEED OF MERCY. The words
were as silent as seeds opening one at a time in his
blood.
When finally he raised himself, the burning bush had
disappeared. A line of fire ate languidly at the treeline
and here and there a thin crest of flame rose farther
back in the woods where a dull red cloud of smoke had
gathered. The boy stopped and picked up a handful of
dirt off his great-uncle's grave and smeared it on his
forehead. Then after a moment, without looking back
he moved across the far field and off the way Buford
had gone.
By midnight he had left the road and the burning
woods behind him and had come out on the highway
once more. The moon, riding low above the field beside him, appeared and disappeared, diamond bright,
between patches of darkness. Intermittently the boy's
jagged shadow slanted across the road ahead of him as
if it cleared a rough path toward his goal. His singed
eyes, black in their deep sockets, seemed already to envision the fate that awaited him but he moved steadily
on, his face set toward the dark city, where the children of God lay sleeping.[1]

In the final chapter of *The Violent Bear It Away*, Flannery O'Connor assumes the narrative stance of an omniscient author. She observes a scene, noting details of surroundings that the
crazed boy would not have noticed himself—there is a red streak
where earth and sky meet; the moonlight shifts among clouds; Tarwater's eyes are black. She charts young Tarwater's movements in
the woods and along the road and allows herself access to his impressions, his new insights, and, indeed, the substance of his "revelation" to "go warn the children of God of the terrible speed of
mercy." While it is clear that Francis Tarwater experiences these
impressions, it is equally clear that he has neither the perspective
nor the expanse of language necessary for such a formulation of
them. It is not his mind that summarizes and selects, and hence it

is no accident that the major images and structural patterns of the novel—fire, hunger, prophecy, broken covenant, and death—coalesce in this final scene. Though she had been less intrusive earlier in the story, O'Connor must have sensed, here, the need for strong and immediate direction of response toward an otherwise powerful but ambiguous novel.

The aim of unabashed "telling" in fiction is unhindered communication. The impulse behind its use at a time when literary taste favors dramatic presentation must be the fear of a reader's misconstruing important events. In effect, this authorial stance recognizes the limitations of Eliot's "objective correlative" or Flaubert's insistence that the phenomenal world properly described contains its own interpretation. When the natural world, or in this instance the supernatural world, does not speak unambiguously for itself, the writer's discipline of self-forgetful absorption in his subject does not evoke a clear emotional response. It invites confusion.

So, O'Connor's tendency here in these last paragraphs, born of distrust and urgency, is to manipulate the reader's attitudes by direct comment and to use the substance of the natural world for specific effect and with conscious distortion. Although it is possible to infer from the previous fictional events, dialogue between characters, and allusion, that young Tarwater is vainly struggling to wrench himself away from his designation as a contemporary prophet, we are told so explicitly. "He felt it building from the blood of Abel to his own, rising and engulfing him. . . . He knew that this was the fire that had encircled Daniel, that had raised Elijah from the earth, that had spoken to Moses and would in the instant speak to him." Unfortunately, the asserted link between Tarwater's enlightenment and that of the Old Testament prophets does not settle the central interpretive question of the novel: do we witness in this act of identification the consummation or the destruction of a life?

The critical problems are manifold. Many commentators assume that the end of the novel is, in fact, a beginning, that the young boy, purged by violence and possessing a new spiritual imperative, will begin his appointed mission. Stuart L. Burns writes, "Smearing his forehead with a 'handful of dirt off his great-uncle's grave,' he sets out once again from Powderhead, this time as a prophet rather than a rebel." And Clinton W. Trowbridge concurs, noting that "he has become one with his great-uncle; and accepting his call as prophet, returns."[2] There are, however, reasons to doubt these optimistic appraisals of Tarwater's renewal.

Far from rendering an apotheosis, the novel's ending imparts what was inevitable from the first. Tarwater's assumption of his role as prophet was feared and forestalled, but it was anticipated.

> The Lord had seen fit to guarantee the purity of his up-bringing, to preserve him from contamination, to preserve him as his elect servant, trained by a prophet for prophecy.
>
> . . . .
>
> He stood like one condemned, waiting at the spot of execution. Then the revelation came, silent, implacable, direct as a bullet. . . . He only knew, with a certainty sunk in despair, that he was expected to baptize the child he saw and begin the life his great-uncle had prepared him for. He knew that he was called to be a prophet and that the ways of his prophecy would not be remarkable. (17, 91)

The revelation that hovers between the red-gold tree of fire and the great-uncle's grave is the command that old Tarwater, arms flailing, had issued repeatedly during the boy's backwoods upbringing. What has changed is the boy's receptiveness to the words. Again, there is a critical dilemma, for the drama of the novel has been played until now upon a stage of resistance. The strength of young Tarwater's character has been measured by "a passion equal and opposite to the old man's" (35). By the only standards the boy has established for himself (and the author has failed to establish an alternative norm by which we might reverse Tarwater's standard and see self-abnegation as a virtue), his prophecy begins with self-defeat.

Considered in this light, the novel presents Tarwater as the particular victim of psychological determinism. Prophecy is not of positive value but is merely an obsession inculcated in youth. O'Connor, however, was quick to anticipate this viewpoint and to try to discredit it. "Tarwater is certainly free and meant to be; if he appears to have a compulsion to be a prophet, I can only insist that in this compulsion there is the mystery of God's will for him, and that it is not a compulsion in the clinical sense."[3] But support for a deterministic reading comes directly from the novel. "An insight came to [Rayber] that he was not to question until the end. He understood that the boy was held in bondage by his great-uncle, that he suffered a terrible false guilt for burning and not burying him" (106). While O'Connor's personal antipathy toward rationalists like Rayber can be surmised from the attitudes of philosophers whom she admired and from her own letters to friends, the credibility of this way of thinking cannot be immediately dismissed here; rather, its validity is precisely what is to be determined by inferring the structure and values of an infrafictional moral universe.[4] Unless the information necessary to deduce such a set of values is contained in the prose, it is impossible to assume any particular attitude toward the fictive events. Certainly it is not warranted to espouse the position of the artist, and to assume, a priori, that the world of the novel is the world of the writer's own life. To do so is to credit fiction only as an expressive extension of a writer's personal code and to deny it any meaning independent of private connotation. As J. V. Cunningham has pointed out, "Insofar as the meaning is not expressed in or recoverable from the statements, the work of art is deficient."[5] There is evidence, in brief, that Tarwater's appointed mission at the end of the story may simply be the fruit of irreversible psychological damage.

The issue of judging the worth of Tarwater's final prophecy can be further clarified by considering it in conditional form. Because the values of the novel, the particular bent of its moral perspective, are inextricably bound to our assessment of old Tarwater's teaching, the truth or bias of his statements affects the evaluation of all subsequent fictive events. Both young Tarwater and Rayber define themselves and act with reference to this old backwoodsman. The consideration can be posed in this way: if old Tarwater was mad, then the boy has, in becoming a prophet, also succumbed to madness. The converse is: if old Tarwater was divinely inspired, then the boy has returned from a mistaken and rebellious effort at an alternative life-style to a higher order of wisdom. Establishing the validity of the first part of the proposition will lead to a fairly certain conclusion, and indeed, this is in one sense the central inquiry of young Tarwater himself. As he hitchhikes into the city, he articulates the purpose of his journey. "My great-uncle learnt me everything, but first I have to find out how much of it is true" (79).

O'Connor's manipulation of sympathy toward old Tarwater can thus be considered a crucial strategy, and it is one that she handled in an interesting way. The old man, dead from the book's first sentence, is seen only in memory, first through the eyes of the boy he sought to influence, then from the vantage of Rayber, the city-bred nephew he hated. The implications of this technique of interference are notable, for Mason Tarwater's presentation is constantly modulated by other characters' particular interest in seeing him. The process of finding a valid perspective on the old man becomes, then, an indirect one. Nonetheless, this fictional procedure does permit the discovery that many of the old man's judgments were accurate; and because the fictional representation of memory inevitably juxtaposes past to present, the old man's influence is felt to be immediate.

There is, most prominently, old Tarwater's insistence that Rayber loved him as he would love a father and had never been able to escape his influence. His proud assertion, "Me, I never left his mind. I had taken my seat in it" (66), is later confirmed by the nephew's own admission, "You infected me with your idiot hopes, your foolish violence. I'm not always myself" (73), and by his stricken look, "painful and awful," at news of the old man's death. That the self-styled prophet affected Rayber is not to be questioned, but neither is it a central critical insight. More important is the attitude one is asked to take toward his powerful and primitive Christianity, and the grounds for judgment on this issue are obscure. Pitted against old Tarwater's singular, spirited insistence on the truth of his own message are the opinions of other characters. For one example, Rayber "always felt with it a rush of longing to have the old man's eyes—insane, fish-colored, violent with their impossible vision of a world transfigured—turned on him once again. The longing was like an undertow in his blood dragging him backwards to what he knew to be madness" (114). The influence of prophetic religion, in this instance, is felt to be pernicious, a compulsion that is overcome only by continual effort. In fact, the most compelling measure of Mason Tarwater's strength might be considered a negative one, illustrated by the energy Rayber expends in trying to escape him. Young Tarwater's struggle is similar, signaled repeatedly in the narrative by assertions that "he ain't had no effect on me." "I'm free" (103). It is clear, at least to Rayber, that this is false, that the old man had transferred his fixation to the boy; and his own attempt, a prolonged appeal to reason, is to convince Tarwater to espouse the rudiments of rational conduct. The boy, in turn, fights that appeal: "I'm free. I'm outside your head. I ain't in it and I ain't about to be" (111).

There is established, then, a complicated system of interpersonal relations and, growing from that, an equally complex pattern of comment and cross comment by characters who seek to influence each other and equally to escape influence. Being "seated inside" someone else's head, being in any way directed or affected by another person, seems to be one of the book's prime evils. The various perspectives are handled in the narrative by Faulknerian shifts of consciousness. The author allows herself consecutive access to one perceiving mind and then another. This works to establish a value system and confer validity on opinion only when several perspectives concur. For example, the certainty of the boy's emotional bondage, despite his struggle for independence, is not disputed. Both Rayber and Tarwater have the same insight about this. But at other times, the effect of multiple shifts of consciousness is one of moral ambiguity. While we know Flannery O'Connor's personal view—that religion offers the only viable and live alternative to the sterile rationalism of contemporary life—the problem for her fiction is that the conflict between spiritual life and rational life, as encountered dramatically, is real. Although Rayber is characterized as a vapid and emotionally stunted man, his perspective is plausible and probably the more so for many readers because its secularism accords with their preexisting attitudes.[6] O'Connor knew that her readers would identify with him. To reject those attitudes (the novel asks for radical realignment of vision; it is not a book that nudges gently and augments quiet insights) the narrative "argument" for the prophetic viewpoint must be decisive.

But decision is precisely what is lacking. Instead of presenting old Tarwater's perspective as the clearly virtuous one, O'Connor hedges, and this hesitancy has serious consequences. One can speculate on the source of her difficulty. The "monstrous reader," the author's ever-present audience, might not only be dense but offended. He might not easily believe in prophecy and the message of religious enlightenment. Consequently the resisting point of view must be anticipated and dramatized within the work itself.[7] This was, as O'Connor realized, a crucial narrative strategy, and it was one that she initially had trouble managing. To Catharine Carver, who read her unpublished manuscript and suggested that the Rayber section be strengthened, O'Connor replied: "Rayber has been the difficulty all along. I'll never manage to get him as alive as Tarwater and the old man but I can certainly improve on him. . . . [Robert Fitzgerald] said essentially the same thing you have, so that corroborates it. He put it this way: be sure you haven't made too much of a parody of Rayber, as if you do, you take away from the point and significance of what Tarwater sees."[8]

In pursuit of this strategy, with the intent to acknowledge and thereby contain the nonspiritual, O'Connor makes characters comment negatively both on old Tarwater and on the boy when he is acting according to his backwoods upbringing. There is, of course, Rayber. "It had taken him barely half a day to find out that the old man had made a wreck of the boy" (97), and Rayber's repeated comment on old Tarwater that "he was a mad-man" (104). There is also the copper flue salesman. "What Meeks had decided after about a half hour of the boy was that he was just enough off in the head and just ignorant enough to be a good worker" (54). And there is young Tarwater himself. "The boy sensed that this was the heart of his great-uncle's madness, this hunger [for the bread of life]" (21). He concludes of the old man: "He was crazy! He was crazy! That's the long and short of it, he was crazy!" (44). And he judges his alter ego. "He was aware of another figure who had fancied himself destined at the moment to the torture of prophecy. It was apparent to the boy that this person . . . was mad" (222). These excerpts from the novel all support the opinion that Mason Tarwater and his nephew are crazy. It is reasonable to think that Flannery O'Connor wrote them from a desire to convince her readers that she too perceived the deficiencies in her characters; but by indulging her desire not to offend, she has lost the ability unambiguously to affect. Giving voice to a secular (*i.e.*, psychological) perspective in the fiction has done more than pay lip service to it. It has presented the reader with grounds for a moral choice. Old Tarwater may be just what he seems—insane. It should be clear that the author's use of multiple, privileged narrative stances is problematic. Because O'Connor has allowed herself equal access to each of several dissenting minds, sympathy for each is potentially the same.

To see an alternative way of managing sympathy, compare O'Connor's fiction to Jane Austen's, in which a delicately balanced narrative distance is maintained through a prolonged inside view of one flawed but basically "good" consciousness. The sheer weight of access to one narrative perspective assures a reader's affinities. As Wayne Booth has commented in his essay on *Emma*, the mixture of sympathy and condemnation that Emma's conduct evokes is the result of a very careful manipulation.[9] By seeing Emma and the events of the story from the girl's perspective, the emotional as well as the moral and intellectual distance between reader and fictional character is reduced. Identification replaces judgment, and sympathy is moderated only by establishing a behavioral norm elsewhere in the text (in Mr. Knightly's behavior and admonitions) that Emma fails to meet.

O'Connor makes no such biased appeal to sympathy. Each central character is equally accessible, or to be more accurate, equally inaccessible; for the portrayal of character in this novel is, in effect, a portrayal of monomania. Subtlety of personality, complication of motive, such as one would find in an Austen or James novel, are nonexistent. O'Connor writes instead with a steady and flat insistence on what is driven or obsessive in human personality. Her privileged access to the "underhead" (as she puts it) of each central consciousness divulges unilinear sources of thought and emotional response.

Even psychic conflict is presented as the self divided almost literally in two, with the lines of contention clearly, rigidly defined.[10] With chilling clarity of mind, Rayber sees himself "divided in two— a violent and a rational self." His conduct usually proceeds from a studied program to subdue any of the irrational impulses of his nature. The most obvious schizoid behavior is apparent in young Tarwater, whose conflict is externalized by rendering his thought as a dialogue between identifiable speakers. The source of this technique is O'Connor's literal transcription of an observation in Emmanuel Mournier's *The Character of Man.* "When we say that thought is dialogue, we mean this quite strictly. We never think alone. The unspoken thought is a dialogue with someone who questions, contradicts or spurs one on." Undoubtedly O'Connor called Tarwater's second "voice" into use as an indication of the richness of his internal resources. She commented in the margins of her copy of Mournier's book, "Rayber's thought has ceased to be dialogue—no voice answers him, no voice questions."[11] But its use does not suggest depth of perception or the darkness of unexplored psyche; rather, it places the conflict on an obvious plane of statement and counterstatement. Doubt is articulated, and in the clarity of its enunciation, it loses a sense of mystery. Pitted against Tarwater's awe of Mason Tarwater, and his dutiful motions to give him the requested Christian burial, is an impulse to renounce the whole content of his uncle's isolated and inglorious religion. The second voice points out that the dead are poor, that old Tarwater was foolish, childish, "crazy all along." It goads him to burn the great-uncle's remains and mockingly reminds him that he has never been "called." In one sense, it is the voice of reason and a strong and heretofore suppressed aspect of the boy's character; alternatively, it is the tempter, the source of religious doubt, the destroyer of faith. Regardless of the content of these admonitions, it is important to notice that they are fully externalized. Psychological processes receive the same treatment as dramatic encounter. Nothing remains hidden and unexpressed.

For a writer who designated her central concern to be with mystery, this is an interesting technique. It deviates markedly from the writing style of the biblical narrators who wrote about Tarwater's prototypes, the Old Testament prophets. As Erich Auerbach has pointed out, the stories of these biblical men's lives are fraught with "background"; they are tempered and haunted by a sense of concealed meaning.[12] The impression of depth and of various layers of consciousness is effected in several ways. The most prominent characteristic of the writing is the paucity of sensory description. Far from resulting in a flaccid story, this sparseness adds dimension. Omission has its positive uses, primarily because it establishes a discrepancy between the skeletal events of a narrative and a dense texture of meaning: the unstated invites investigation. To give an example, the book of Jonah, in four brief chapters, records the central episodes of a prophet's life: his resistance to God's command, the strangeness of God's consequent punishment, Jonah's change of heart and obedience, and his final confusion at God's use of his prophecy. To be called to prophesy destruction of a civilization, to be swallowed by a whale, then to have the prophecy negated by God's apparently fickle purpose, are events of unqualified drama in any life. Yet the trauma of Jonah's experience is never made explicit. The events are told simply, with no heightened rhetorical effect, with no reference to his emotions except finally his articulation of a wish to die. God gives his command in direct discourse and Jonah responds—first to resist, then to succumb. Only so much of the phenomenon as is necessary for the purpose of the narrative is externalized. We know nothing of the city except that it is called Nineveh and is evil, nothing of the prophet's character, nothing of time. The effect of these omissions is to throw the focus of response back toward the interpretation of the fictional events: Jonah is important insofar as he embodies God's will; Nineveh is named only because it has violated God's intended mode of human conduct.

How radically different this mode of presentation is from O'Connor's rendering of a calling. The difference acquires significance when one recalls that Jonah, a subject of frequent allusion in *The Violent Bear It Away*, is considered to be a biblical analogue for young Tarwater. The biblical seer moves distantly, mysteriously, viewed by his biographer as an inscrutable puppet whose rebellion is briefly countenanced by God. The Lord speaks directly and actively intrudes to shape the course of Jonah's life. By contrast, the human life portrayed in O'Connor's story is completely open. There is no reason to look behind the fictive events for their interpretation; the surface realities are complete in themselves. Either thoughts are dramatized (Tarwater's second voice) or the author assumes a privileged stance so that the contents of consciousness are revealed anyway. Although O'Connor consciously cultivated it as an effect, mystery, even the mystery of human sensibility, is dissipated by externalization. None of the conscious omissions used so pointedly by the Old Testament writers of prophecy suggest concealed meanings in O'Connor's narrative art.

A second valuable point of comparison between this modern teller of spiritual tales and the Old Testament writers involves a curious reversal; for despite the lack of specificity that is noted as a general quality of biblical narratives, God is actively present and effective in the lives of his chosen people. The book of Jonah begins, "Now the word of the Lord came unto Jonah . . . saying." The ensuing action is in effect a dialogue between God and his servant, a conversation in which the Lord's silence and withdrawal are as positively felt as his direct commands. Although it is problematic to call this God a character in any conventional sense—he is mysterious, disembodied, identified only by his voice—he appears directly and unambiguously, and engenders clearly recognizable human responses. Alternatively, in *The Violent Bear It Away*, all of young Tarwater's spiritual imperatives come from his great-uncle. Even the last "Go tell the children of God" is heard with the boy's ear to the earth of the uncle's grave. Dramatically it is feasible to think that the command is a reiteration in memory of the old man's previous instructions, and this indirection opens the possibility of a subjective, fanatical interpretation of the event. In the same way that Mason Tarwater is seen indirectly, biased in presentation by the boy's quirks and Rayber's rationalizations, so God is experienced through the teachings of an old man who may be mad. He has no independent existence, even as a dramatic influence on the boy; the influence is always Mason Tarwater's. It is precisely the lack of dramatization that leads to ambiguity in this instance.

We are left with no definitive set of norms in this novel. The manipulation of attitude toward Tarwater and the boy is complex, but ultimately it fails to provide clear guidance. The old man and his great-nephew are rendered with the same flatness, the same degree of externalization as Rayber. No additional authorial comment, insight, or dramatic access to their perceptions lend them superior claim to a reader's support. Instead of selecting a single, specific angle of observation, O'Connor branches into varied, subjective perspectives that compositely lead to ambiguity rather than certainty of interpretation.

With a similar ambivalence, she often fails to bias narrative description, mismanaging an otherwise subtle and pervasive opportunity to approve or discredit characters and actions. I am not talking here of the uses of epithets of the kind baldly employed by Homer ("How could I ever forget the admirable Odysseus? He is not only the wisest man alive but has been the most generous in his offerings") and less blatantly but to the same effect by early, unabashedly intrusive narrators like Fielding or Austen ("Emma

Woodhouse, handsome, clever, and rich, with a comfortable home and happy disposition, seemed to unite some of the best blessings of existence").[13] Such direct authorial comment has been held in disregard in modern times. In 1938 R. G. Collingwood warned against its use in *The Principles of Art*, as did Ortega y Gasset, who felt that an author should "furnish the visible facts" that allow a reader to discover and imaginatively define values for himself.[14] Attuned to the critical canons of her contemporaries, O'Connor was careful in her use of descriptions. They are not offered in a specifically normative way, but norms can be inferred from them nonetheless. Consider, for example, the initial meeting of Rayber and young Tarwater. "He had thrust on the black-rimmed glasses and he was sticking a metal box into the waist band of his pajamas. This was joined by a cord to the plug in his ear. For an instant the boy had the thought that his head ran by electricity. He caught Tarwater by the arm and pulled him into the hall under a lantern-shaped light that hung from the ceiling. The boy found himself scrutinized by two small drill-like eyes set in the depth of twin glass caverns" (87–88). The semblance of objective narration is initially convincing. More careful reflection suggests that objectivity is suspect, that O'Connor the storyteller has metaphorized herself into a focal character, so that her observations are apparently no more comprehensive than young Tarwater's. Employing such a technique at this point—a third-person narration siphoned through the consciousness of a central figure—precludes establishing more than a skeleton of objective reality. Rayber put on his glasses and hearing aid to look at his nephew. Embellishing the description of this simple act are the meanings these mechanical aids have for the untutored boy. In his ignorance he thinks not that his uncle is deaf and needs assistance to hear, but that the man's entire mind is dependent on an external source of energy.

The effects of this fictional strategy are complicated. Although what is given is actually a highly circumscribed point of view, the description of Rayber acts effectively to convey value. Inevitably the reader as well as the country boy sees this schoolteacher as a mechanically programmed human being. In this case, the use of naïve commentary renders strange what might otherwise be accepted. The ordinary (here the hearing aid) becomes unfamiliar and threatening. What is normally taken for granted attains a narrative stature that demands critical attention.

This technique provides an excellent tool for manipulating value. The limited point of view that notices and relates the details of Rayber's appearance allows O'Connor to avoid direct authorial comment while still articulating a moral repulsion against obsessive rationality. There is a perspective from which Rayber's intelligence can be seen as run by machinery. Fearing spontaneity, he lives according to a battery of ideas and measuring devices for human conduct.

The problem is that this technique is not used discriminately. Almost all description of character is siphoned through intelligence of a very peculiar bent. Old Tarwater is as alien as his nephew. "He was a bull-like old man with a short head set directly into his shoulders and silver protruding eyes that looked like two fish straining to get out of a net of red threads" (10). This portrait of Mason Tarwater is given at the moment preceding his death. It is known without question that this is his great-nephew's perspective: "Tarwater, sitting across the table from him, saw." Although the boy's vision is the occasion for noting old Tarwater's appearance, the descriptive terms are incongruous. A country youth may view humanity metaphorically in terms of animals, but it is no accident, in a novel whose controlling purpose is evaluation of "loaves and fishes," that is, of the miraculous in human life, that the old man's eyes look like fish. The source of the image is disguised, but it is finally, unmistakably O'Connor's own formulation.

We have, then, several descriptions purporting to be objective but revealing on further consideration the bias of subjective viewpoint. These descriptions are nonetheless maneuvered by the author for ulterior purposes. In the first instance the motive is to make

Rayber seem alien and ridiculous; in the second, it is to ally old Tarwater's person with the boy's search for either material or spiritual
sustenance. But it should be observed that the second description
is very much like the first, particularly in one respect: some aspect
of physical appearance is made to appear grotesque. Rayber's eyes
are "small, drill-like, set in the depth of twin glass caverns" (88).
Old Tarwater's eyes "looked like two fish straining to get out of a
net of red threads" (10). If we bear these similarities in mind, what
textual evidence suggests that Tarwater is a holy man and Rayber a
fool? The question is rhetorical, for the descriptions of both are
equally alienating. It is impossible to infer from them that one of the
men enacts or represents a norm of behavior and value, while the
other deviates from it. If any inference is to be drawn, the most accurate one would seem to be that neither man is attractive, and indeed the predominant impression conveyed by the novel is that all
of humanity is unspeakably gross.

To return to the events that close the novel after these various considerations of imperfectly controlled allegiance is to return to un-
certainties. The grounds for unambiguous interpretation simply
have not been firmly laid. It is not entirely a matter of knowing
whether young Tarwater is a latter-day prophet—he is. The pattern
of allusion in the book is too explicit to misinterpret. Elijah, Elisha,
Moses, Daniel, Jonah, are all tucked in and around the narrative of
Tarwater's four-day trial and finally, unquestionably make their
claim. Nor is it a problem of understanding imagery. The loaves and
fishes that fed the hungry multitude in the Bible story are set up as
one pole of a dramatic tension between spiritual and material sustenance.[15] Barbecued sandwiches and dried, cartoned cereals vie
with the Bread of Life for Tarwater's life. Initially he vomits up the
one and eschews the other, but his final insight is unmistakable.
"The boy too leaned forward, aware at last o. the object of his hunger, aware that it was the same as the old man's and that nothing on
earth would fill him" (241). In both image and allusion we are told

that Tarwater, in spite of all his previous contrary energy, has opted for the spiritual life. But if his decision is certain, the consequences of it are not.

By all the canons of realism that O'Connor purported to espouse, a boy who has not eaten for four days and whose worms prevent him from stomaching any food is surely near the point of death. In addition, having murdered an idiot child, set fire to a wilderness, and been molested and raped, he is almost certainly mad. O'Connor records not only a spiritual election but the prescience of death when she writes: "His scorched eyes no longer looked hollow or as if they were meant only to guide him forward. They looked as if touched with a coal like the lips of the prophet, they would never be used for ordinary sights again" (233).

This is not the usual understanding of the outcome of Tarwater's trial, but other textual evidence besides an appeal to the precepts of realism suggest this to be a plausible interpretation.[16] Despite the desperate issue of individual freedom and young Tarwater's efforts to remain "outside of [everybody's] head," the training of his youth is finally determining and secures his allegiance to Mason Tarwater. His final "vision" is, then (to borrow Auerbach's term), a *figura*. In the text, the relation between the old man and his nephew has been described explicitly as that between Elijah and Elisha, the younger man destined to "receive the mantle of prophecy" from Elijah on his death. Even if the implications of the allusion are not understood, it is clear that young Tarwater's life is prefigured in the life of his dead uncle. Old Tarwater had "been called in his early youth and had set out for the city to proclaim the destruction awaiting a world that had abandoned its savior" (5). Young Tarwater, "his singed eyes, black in their deep sockets, seemed already to envision the fate that awaited him, *but* he moved steady on, his face set toward the dark city where the children of God lay sleeping" (243). If the repeated circumstance of calling has predictive value in the narrative, the old man's prophecy of earthly destruction by "blood and fire" would foreshadow the effectiveness of the boy's mission. Ma-

son Tarwater's prediction was empty. "One morning he saw to his
joy, a finger of fire coming out of it, and before he could turn, before
he could shout, the finger had touched him and the destruction he
had been waiting for had fallen in his own brain and his own body.
His blood had been burned dry and not the blood of the world" (5–
6). There is no reason to believe that young Tarwater's vision is
different from this dark insight about personal mortality. It is the
self that will certainly be destroyed, and the boy is well on his way
to that end, as O'Connor herself knew. "Now about Tarwater's future. He must of course not live to realize his mission, but die to
realize it. The children of God I daresay will dispatch him pretty
quick. Nor am I saying that he has a great mission or that God's solution for the problems of our particular world are prophets like Tarwater. Tarwater's mission might only be to baptize a few more idi-
ots." [17] This reading of the text is supported by the grammar of the
last sentence of the novel, which established an opposition between Tarwater's vision of his own fate and his return to the city.
He envisioned a curtailed personal future, *but* he moved forward.
He does not go back in consequence of insight, but in spite of it.

Considered in this manner, the nature of the boy's spiritual imperative—"Go warn the children of God of the terrible speed of
mercy"—becomes less cryptic. To the secular reader, mercy has a
very particular meaning, and inevitably one asks what divine clem-
ency or kindness has been experienced by Tarwater and what will
then constitute the substance of his prophetic message. As far as it
is possible reasonably to surmise, he has seen the inevitability of his
own death, and whether he proclaims this vision is irrelevant. The
events of the narrative suggest that revelation is private and occasioned by holocaust. Short of violence, the individual, and certainly
society as a whole, can resist the uncomfortable awareness of the
end of human life.

With the meaning of these last crucial narrative events clarified,
the central interpretive question still remains: has the boy been
saved or damned? The issue is obscured not only by the ambiguity

of this last scene but by what has immediately preceded it—the
baptism-murder of the idiot boy, Bishop. As Ruth Vande Kieft observes, what is morally shocking in this action is not that the moment of murder should coincide with the presumed moment of
grace (as it would in any religious martyrdom), but that "murder
should almost appear to become the means of a sacrament, since,
given Tarwater's divided state, his obsession both to kill and to baptize, the sacrament could not have been otherwise administered." [18]
Death under ordinary circumstances is regarded as fearful or tragic.
For an author to maneuver her subject so that his end can be
viewed positively only if the reader can accept self-defeat as vic-
tory, death as mercy, sacrament as blasphemy, and murder as incon-
sequential, is a notable fictional achievement, but also a puzzling
one.

One can speculate about the reasons for this strategy. It is the
work of a writer fatally ill from the time of her maturity, a woman
who claimed that "death [was] brother to [her] imagination" but
who was most comfortably able to assume the mask of public joke-
ster, even in her own life and about matters of crucial seriousness
to her.[19] When she wrote to Robert Fitzgerald after her first bout
with lupus, she mentioned no pain or fears; instead she conceded
lightly, "I am doing fairly well these days though I am practically
bald headed on top and have a watermelon face." [20] She apparently
found comfort in obscuring her awful and omnipresent awareness
of disease with the distance of humor. Comedy and terror coin-
cided in her imagination. For someone so plagued, death *was* mer-
ciful; for one who held tenaciously to an orthodox religious perspective, death was not only the end of suffering but an entry into
eternity.

But the concerns of a life and the excellences of fiction writing
do not necessarily coincide. An author's belief enters into fiction
only insofar as it is written into it. Not only must literal events be
presented unambiguously, but attitudes toward those events must
be aligned so that, for the purposes of reading, the audience knows

how to regard what it has encountered. This is not a matter of assuming a shared sensibility with an audience, but of creating a value system within the fiction which functions as an intrinsic guide.

Did she succeed in the case before us? In an article published four years after her death, Stuart Burns argued, "In a world in which the eminently plausible and sweet voice of reason turns out to be the dragon of perverted seduction and betrayal, madness (if one wishes so to call the prophetic vision) is a necessary adjunct to salvation."[21] But in *The Violent Bear It Away*, the prophetic vision is presented in no more attractive a light than its alternative. Speaking privately to a friend, O'Connor offered the opinion that "truth does not change according to our ability to stomach it emotionally." She felt that the truth "as revealed by faith [could be] hideous, emotionally disturbing, down-right repulsive."[22] And that is what she has chosen to dramatize in her novel: the suffering rather than the blessings of religious faith. Young Tarwater's choices are "hideous, emotionally disturbing" because he must choose between the extremes of an emotional attraction so strong that it is insane by the world's standards and a dry intellectual repression of the irrational. Moreover, precisely because every potentially supernatural event in the novel is provided with an adequate rational explanation (the boy's unappeasable hunger is caused by worms; the burning tree stands in the midst of a man-made fire), the reader is given no unanswerable evidence favoring the prophetic vision as an explanation of those events and in fact is left to see both of the boy's alternatives as unpalatable and very likely unlivable.

But if the story itself does not adequately cue the reader's sympathies, then the final meaning must remain ambiguous. Such ambiguity may be entirely proper; few readers would want a "moral" that could be lifted from the text and would, in summing it up, eliminate a facile interpretation. But by the same token, however much it succeeds on other counts—and it does—this powerful, haunting novel fails as anagogical fiction. The text offers no literal discrepancy or omission to force an appeal to a "higher, hidden order."[23] And though the reader may be willing to suspend disbelief, to enter for the time being into some special value system of the novel, the intrinsic evidence does not permit him to discover what those values are. The problem of anagogical fiction is one of cognition, not of belief. Despite O'Connor's evident desires, *The Violent Bear It Away* remains a secular novel because its fictional constructs invite secular, that is, realistic, explanations which, intentionally or not, suffice.

SIX

Epiphany

And this, as I could not prevail on any of my actors to
speak, I was obliged to declare myself.

Henry Fielding
Tom Jones

I

Flannery O'Connor never wrote a first-person narrative,
nor did she ever completely surrender her third-person prose to
the limitations of a subjective point of view. She undertook the
offices of writer with all the freedoms of traditional storytelling, assuming the omniscient manipulation of fictional destinies with an
unquestioning ease. One wonders if she could have written otherwise, for a subjective perspective in fiction writing narrows the authority of the given account; it implies that there can be another
point of view, a different set of meanings to assigned events. In turn,
this relativity suggests that one can live in doubt, that one can live,
as Lionel Trilling has said, "by means of a question" instead of by an
unassailable religious persuasion.[1]

This was exactly what O'Connor did not want to do—to concede
that there could be more than one viable interpretation of reality.
In her opinion, conflicts between ways of being constituted a chal-
lenge to Christian truth that could not be brooked, and with this
certainty of outlook, she reserved final narrative authority for herself. For the hard of hearing she would "shout," for the blind she
would "draw large and startling figures."[2] Yet with all this allusion
to rhetoric, to bold and unambiguous fictional strategies, O'Connor

was curiously reluctant to exploit the potential of the omniscient voice. Rarely in all these tales of bizarre and violent experience does she reflect on the meaning of the grotesquery or give explicit value to fictional events. She infrequently enunciates in her fictional world what she had no trouble conveying in personal life—that Christian orthodoxy was the consistent measure of experience. This is usually left for the reader to infer, to come upon through the indirections of allusion, incongruities, and distorted hyperbole.

As must be clear by now, I have the image of O'Connor creating her audience from her own fears and isolation, creating a composite image from antagonistic reviews that arrived in the mail, conjuring a reader who was not only ignorant but, like so many of the characters of her own imagination, resistant to her theological point of view. Any author as removed from live, intelligent, and informed readership as O'Connor was must evolve a complicated kind of "double-think" to deal with this distance. As Martha Stephens has noticed, "Flannery O'Connor seems to have sought, all her writing life, a means of approach to an audience whose religious sense she believed to be stunted and deformed."[3] She thought as a Christian and wrote as a Christian while constantly second-guessing her "monstrous reader," anticipating the workings of a mind that did not know by experience or explicit heritage the forms and assumptions of Christianity. But I would like to suggest that to "shout" in fiction about any belief, Christian or otherwise, is done effectively, not by leaving norms or opinions implicit in the text, reachable if at all through inference, but by interpreting events explicitly, through the privileges of the omnisciently narrated tale, or by making man's encounter with religion the explicit topic of exposition. There is a limit to what one can infer from a text, just as there is a limit to what can be accepted in writing. It was in the precarious territory where one neither offended nor obscured by excessive indirection that I think O'Connor tried to live artistically.

Perhaps O'Connor's reluctance to take full advantage of the possibilities of omniscient narration was the result of her own "double-thinking," her anxiety that hostile readers or astute critics would take offense at open preachments; perhaps it arose in response to her own belief that dramatization is a more effective narrative procedure than straight address to the reader. She was unlike Graham Greene, who had the same concern to manipulate judgment but did not hesitate to comment directly when he sensed, in *Brighton Rock*, for example, that readers might apply the conventional standards of right and wrong rather than the required standards of good and evil. He distinguished carefully between the pitiable but blessed "hole" where Rose lived, knowing "murder, copulation, extreme poverty, fidelity and the love and fear of God," and the glaring "open world outside" where people like Ida made a false claim to experience.[4] Whatever the source of her reticence, O'Connor tried most often simply to enact the experience of revelation in her fiction, hoping that the implications of dramatized events would be self-evident. However, the limitations on a reader's understanding of these revelations is imposed directly by her handling of them. For time and again—in "Greenleaf," "Good Country People," "A Circle in the Fire," "Parker's Back," "A View of the Woods"—the protagonist is taken to the point of profound insight and then is killed or simply abandoned by an author who apparently fears that denouement will lessen the impact of undeniably dramatic events. The reader is left, then, with a burden, with a brooding sense of weight, of ominous importance whose source is ultimately ambiguous, unlocatable in clearly defined experience. For as talented as O'Connor is at rendering the violent and profound moment, she is nonetheless unable or unwilling to dramatize states of consciousness, to take her readers inside the mind of the perceiving character and show them what exactly has been experienced. Virginia Woolf thought this was unimportant. Katharine in the novel *Night and Day* remarks that it is "the process of discovering" that matters, "not the discovery itself."[5] But this cannot be said of O'Connor, for whom, presumably, the content of the revelation was everything. As the following discussion will show, the revelation of epiphany that occurs outside a specifically theological fictional context is left open to a variety of interpretations ("Revelation"), and the revelation that occurs within the parameters of religious quest can still be unsatisfactory ("Parker's Back"). It is only when the author takes it upon herself to expose the thoughts and perceptions of characters in the presence of grace that an unequivocal meaning is accessible to the reader. Although O'Connor may have feared this authorial direction, her infrequent assumption of the role of commentator results in some of the finest passages in her work. For we have at these rare moments a sense of character rendered with sympathy and gladness; human beings are held up in their best hours to be admired instead of judged.

Since the art of any fiction is essentially an art of revelation, some definitions are called for. To begin with, there is a distinction between the gradual disclosure that all stories effect and a revelation to a character that is specific in time and intense in effect. As Morris Beja observes in his book *Epiphany in the Modern Novel*, until the last centuries, *epiphany* identified the moments in which an external force revealed some truth to human beings.[6] But at present the word has come to have a quite different application, especially since it was appropriated by Joyce, who adapted the religious pattern and terminology to secular experience. In *Stephen Hero*, Joyce's autobiographical novel, the author defines his term. Although the passage is familiar and often quoted, it is useful to cite it in this context, if only to contrast it with O'Connor's own understanding of the word. Stephen identifies an epiphany as "a sudden spiritual manifestation, whether in the vulgarity of speech or of gesture or in a memorable phrase of the mind itself. He believed that it was for the man of letters to record these epiphanies, with extreme care, seeing that they themselves are the most delicate and evanescent of moments."[7] Later in the novel Stephen clarifies the idea when he expresses the belief that this manifestation may be produced by "an ordinary concrete object, a work of art, a snatch of talk overheard on the street, a gesture."[8]

Far from being oracular—the voice of a hidden god intruding on the human world—the source of Joyce's epiphany is the human commonplace. Although the stuff of ordinary life occasions sudden illumination, no one may count on such insights. For objects are not "active," impinging forcibly on consciousness. In fact, it is normal to take them for granted. But a sensitive perceiver can effect a transformation, finding suddenly and intuitively the unnoticed value, the hidden meaning. In Joyce's terminology, the artist, the astute perceiver, is a priest who "converts the daily bread of experience into the radiant body of everlasting life."[9] Notice the inversion of the religious concept. Epiphany is no longer a passive human experience—the revelation of a god who is active—as, for example, Paul's revelation and conversion on the Damascus road was passive.[10] Rather, Joyce emphasizes the role of man's mind and imagination. What is revealed is not divinity in the classic sense of an independent deity, but a timeless brilliance previously unperceived; or it is the self that is seen with harsh honesty, as when the boy in "Araby" realizes that his illusions about the fair are not the only ones he has harbored: "Gazing up into the darkness, I saw myself as a creature driven and derided by vanity; and my eyes burned with anguish and anger."[11] In effect, Joyce celebrates the marriage of the sacred and the profane, for the things that are "holy" are precisely those conditions of life that ordinarily seem familiar and squalid. These manifestations are sacred not in a theological sense (deriving from divine grace) but figuratively. Hence the word *spiritual* is used by Joyce only to evoke a sense of submerged meaning, the quality of inner life that is brought to light.

This same celebration of the commonplace is an implicit motive in Virginia Woolf's novel *To the Lighthouse*, and it is also the topic of reflection for at least one of the characters, the painter Lily Briscoe, who observes, "One wishes to feel simply that's a chair, that's a table and yet at the same time, it's a miracle, it's an ecstasy." And at another time, Lily reflects: "The great revelation had never come. The great revelation perhaps never did come. Instead, there were little daily miracles, illuminations, matches struck unexpectedly in the dark."[12]

To both of these authors, the epiphany was evanescent, delicate.

The common things of life were the only components of human experience. Because no larger framework of established meaning existed to lend them weight, the discovery of meaning in the things themselves was the work of creative intelligence. They would have both sympathized with Proust's Marcel, who realized, tasting the madeleine dipped in tea, "It is plain that the object of my quest, the truth, lies not in the cup but in myself." [13]

But O'Connor did not use Joyce or Woolf as her models. For her, Lily Briscoe's "great revelation" did come; in fact, it was the central human experience. All the matches struck in the dark were, by contrast, so many subjective delusions. We can deduce from O'Connor's work her concurrence with the notion that truth is concealed from us except in extraordinary circumstances, but her portrayal of the nature of that truth or the manner of its disclosure reveals a sensibility radically removed from either Joyce's or Woolf's. She seemed to feel more of an affinity with the ancient concept of epiphany, and hence she tended to emphasize a divine movement-human response pattern, whereby people are no longer agents of epiphany through the movements of their minds, but the recipients of some great and even unsought knowledge.

In the fiction these beliefs are recognizable in the narrative patterns of stories. No matter how much an O'Connor protagonist may grumble and bustle about, attending to her fate, the decisive life experience is thrust upon her. A bull rams her; a Negress smashes her; she is captured and shot by a criminal. In all of these tales, the emphasis in the narrative is on human response, on the posture assumed before external force. From this concentration ensues a cumulative sense of human impotence, a suggestion of the inefficacy of self-direction. There is reason to believe that O'Connor understood this passivity to be a virtue. In the introduction to the 1962 edition of *Wise Blood*, she asked rhetorically: "Does one's integrity ever lie in what he is not able to do? I think that it does." [14] And in her letters, she wrote about passive diminishment, about accepting unalterable limitations. But to the reader, this is a disquieting attitude with ambiguous implications.

This sense of life as response rather than action is further reinforced by a rhetorical habit perhaps used unconsciously—a tendency not only to use the passive voice but to describe characters as victims of their own perceptions, as persons accosted by sight and sound rather than simple perceivers. In "Greenleaf," Mrs. May is the target of her own sight; the sun becomes "narrow and pale until it looked like a bullet. Then suddenly it burst through the treeline and raced down the hill toward her." [15] Likewise in "The River," Bevel, drowning in the river, is pursued by the same kind of active vision. "Mr. Paradise's head appeared from time to time on the surface of the water. Finally, far downstream, the old man rose like some ancient water monster and stood empty-handed." [16] If the intention in writing is to create the sense of an unseen, undramatizable divine grace, one way to suggest its presence is certainly through human response to it. Hence the use of passive voice and the intrusion of sight can be regarded as plausible attempts to define by reaction. But again, this is a negative strategy, an acknowledgment that we do not have words for all that is thought to exist. The author "cannot describe what he sees; he can only point to the place where it appears to be." [17] In this circumstance, the audience's expectation of supernatural meaning must be "so strong that a failure within language indicates the reality of something beyond language." [18] The absence of this expectation (and it would be absent in an agnostic readership) leaves room to ascribe various motivations to this general human passivity, especially since O'Connor provides examples of sight violating the onlooker in undoubtedly secular situations, as when Hazel Motes is driving through the country in *Wise Blood*. "The sky leaked over all of it and then began to leak into the car. The head of a string of pigs appeared snout-up over the windowshield and he had to screech to a stop and watch the rear of the last pig disappear shaking into the ditch on the other side." [19] This tendency to use the same technique to represent both potentially religious experience and decidedly nonreligious circumstances parallels O'Connor's use of the grotesque to describe both the "sacred" and the "damned." The indiscriminate use of distorted rendering can result in ambiguous control of a reader's sympathy.[20] In a recent critique, Miles Orvell commented, "It was well that O'Connor had this tradition for it would help her to solve what would be her chief literary problem—how to embody . . . the godly ungrand [quester], the man whose distortion signifies that God, through his grace, is alive in him."[21] But it is difficult to accept this reasoning when ungrand, ungodly men are represented in the same unwieldy terms. Similarly, the perpetually responsive posture of many of these O'Connor characters, religiously obsessed and otherwise, does not lead inevitably to the supposition that their reactions are always to grace but often simply to the conclusion that they are victimized.

The following sections will illustrate these problems as they occur in stories explicitly about the religious experience, or in fictional occasions wherein epiphany (in the old non-Joycean sense of the truth actively revealing itself) is an active principle of storytelling.

II

It is a tribute to O'Connor's "reasonable use of the unreasonable" that, in "Revelation," she could make a bite on a fat woman's neck by a Wellesley student with acne the occasion for self-confrontation. After the attack and before she is drugged, the ugly girl whispers to Mrs. Turpin, "Go back to hell where you come from, you old wart hog!"[22] This farfetched accusation shapes the remaining story, as Mrs. Turpin strives to understand in what sense she can possibly be a pig. "How am I a hog and me both? How am I saved and from hell too?" (506). And, as she ponders these questions, gazing down into the pig parlor on her farm, "as if through the very heart of mystery," the answer comes to her. Her vision is as extraordinary as the events that have preceded it, and it is posed in terms that are equally stark and funny.

> She saw the streak as a vast swinging bridge extending
> upward from the earth through a field of living fire.
> Upon it a vast horde of souls were rumbling toward
> heaven. There were whole companies of white-trash
> clean for the first time in their lives, the bands of black

niggers in white robes, and battalions of freaks and lunatics shouting and clapping and leaping like frogs. And
bringing up the end of the procession was a tribe of
people whom she recognized at once as those who,
like herself and Claud, had always had a little of everything and the God-given wit to use it right. She leaned
forward to observe them closer. They were marching
behind the others with great dignity, accountable as
they had always been for good order and common
sense and respectable behavior. They alone were on
key. Yet she could see by their shocked and altered
faces that even their virtues were being burned away.
She lowered her hands. (508)

As infrequently happens in O'Connor stories, the content of Mrs.
Turpin's revelation is fully externalized; it is made as available to
the reader as to the fictional recipient. Unlike Mrs. May's encounter
in "Greenleaf," or Mrs. Cope's experience at the end of "A Circle in
the Fire," we do not have to construe the probable nature of the
suffering insight. It is a decided step toward rendering of subjective
consciousness; nonetheless, the nature of the vision, even when it is
unmistakably exposed, has its own set of accompanying ambiguities. To understand why, consider the context of this disturbing
revelation.

It is the result of a shock to a respectable woman's self-image.
O'Connor begins the story in a doctor's office, and the patients
waiting for attention constitute a microcosm of southern society.
The chance gathering, the situation of persons unknown to each
other assembled in a room, could provide a forum for discussing
the workings of fate (in the way that Thornton Wilder asks why five
particular people were together on the bridge of San Luis Rey when
it broke), but O'Connor arranges this cast to reflect the workings of
Mrs. Turpin's mind. In this room are all the possibilities of birth and
position in the rural South: a well-dressed, "pleasant" lady; a thin,
worn woman in a cheap cotton dress; another woman in a "gritty-
looking" yellow sweatshirt and slacks; a dirty sniveling child; a fat,

ugly teenager; and eventually a black messenger boy. Her presence in this company occasions one of Mrs. Turpin's frequent reflections on the good fortune of her own position in life, and this extends into the question of who she would have chosen to be if she couldn't have been herself. "If Jesus had said to her before he made her, 'There's only two places available to you. You can either be a nigger or white-trash,' what would she have said?" (491). In the imaginative interior monologue that follows, Mrs. Turpin reveals both the source of her self-satisfaction and her criterion of evaluation: she considers herself a good woman, a hard worker, clean and charitable; she would rather be a black woman with these qualities than "white-trash." When confronted with the imaginative alternative of being born ugly, she is horrified. Although Mrs. Turpin does not articulate these thoughts, O'Connor counterpoints the woman's private musings with what is said, to tell the reader what is actually behind the public facade. For example, when Mrs. Turpin says she and Claud have a pig parlor and a hose to wash down the pigs, she thinks to herself that her animals are cleaner than the snot-nosed child. When a poorly dressed woman says she "wouldn't scoot down no hog with no hose," Mrs. Turpin thinks, "You wouldn't have no hog to scoot down" (494). This discrepancy between private opinion and public comment acts as an effective signal of hypocrisy and shows, without any explicit authorial comment, the distance between Mrs. Turpin's complacency and her faults. Where the woman sees herself as charitable, she is shown to be proud; where she considers herself thoughtful, she is condescending; her solicitousness hides contempt. In terms of both race and class, Mrs. Turpin's self-satisfaction is gained at the expense of others. Although she does not expose herself directly, she insinuates enough for the Wellesley student to surmise the truth, to assault her physically, and to accuse her of being a wart hog.

It is at this juncture that Mrs. Turpin tries to come to terms with the accusation. "'I am not,' she said tearfully, 'a wart hog. From hell'" (502). That the denial has no force shows the protagonist to be moving toward a recognition of the distortion that the reader already has seen. The final vision of souls "rumbling toward heaven" is posed in exactly the terms in which Mrs. Turpin has always seen life, as a matter of social hierarchy. But she envisions herself to be last in line; this time in procession behind the white-trash, Negroes, and lunatics, and it is this image that completes the message of ill-founded self-esteem.

If one wishes to identify grace as that which destroys illusions, then it can be said that Mrs. Turpin has experienced grace. But to say this is very different from making a statement about religion, for the epiphanies that occur in Joyce's fiction can be described in the same way. What is different is the tone and theatricality of O'Connor's moment of insight. In Joyce's work, a young boy looks up at the dim ceiling of a closing fair and says quietly, "I saw myself as a creature driven and derided by vanity." In O'Connor's work, this same realization of vanity is heralded by ponderous machinery. "She raised her hand from the side of the pen in a gesture hieratic and profound. A visionary light settled in her eyes. She saw" (508). The vision that is subsequently revealed is not couched in personal terms; Mrs. Turpin does not see herself as the boy in "Araby" did. She only recognized "those who like herself . . . had always had a little of everything." It should be noticed that the revelation is a dramatization of a hypothetical event—a parade to heaven; it is not the actual statement of understanding. Consequently the abstract meaning of this imaginative parade, both to Mrs. Turpin and to the reader, is still left to be construed. That the march is to heaven and the language theological is undeniable. But the vision occurs in the idiom that has characterized this woman's previous musings; the terms of formulation are consistent with the character of the churchgoing middle class, and in this respect the whole imaginary scene can be considered a metaphor, the concrete terms of an abstraction that remains unstated in the text. The meaning of the vision, then, is not forced into the mold of theology; for the language and images of theology are used as a means to an end that must answer the problems posed in the preceding events of the story. What Mrs. Turpin must see as she turns from the pigsty is her own participation in low life, her own complicity, along with blacks and poor whites, in human suffering and limitation. This is what had remained beyond her self-image in the doctor's waiting room; this is the knowledge that presumably can diminish her complacency. For the reader, the fact that the "message" has been given to Ruby Turpin, "a respectable, hard-working, church-going woman," has its own implications. For it suggests that the most self-respecting people can also be the most dangerous.

III

In the story "Revelation," the secular context of the protagonist's vision served as a guide to the interpretation of that vision. Even if O'Connor had intended that the vision be considered to come from God and to be concerned with Mrs. Turpin's salvation, the evidence is ambiguous. Because the theological norms of behavior are often the norms of society, Mrs. Turpin's faults can be recognized as faults simply by virtue of her deviance from the publicly admired traits of honesty and humility. However, there are occasions when the problems faced in the fictional situation are more specifically religious; one such narrative is "Parker's Back." O'Connor wrote this, her last story, on her deathbed in the Piedmont Hospital, and there is a telling anecdote about the circumstances of its composition. Caroline Gordon went to visit Flannery several weeks before she died and found her weak but cheerfully able to report, as she pulled a pad and pencil from under her pillow, that the doctor wouldn't let her work, but it was all right for her to write a little fiction.[23] The irony of the situation is apparent, as is O'Connor's remarkable and admirable obsession with writing. But these extreme circumstances reveal not only a writer's dedication but her desperation; for the story is contrived, its message offered at the expense of credibility.

The discovery of inconsistency or incompleteness on the literal level of a narrative can lead to a search for meaning on a secondary, nonliteral level of exposition. In "Parker's Back," the realistic inconsistencies of the text are so apparent that it is impossible to follow a "natural symbolism" of events, to construe satisfactorily the inherent meanings of actions. Reference to a value system external to the text is the only way to find any coherence in the narrative, and since the subject of the story is the symbolic representation of God, those meanings are unambiguously religious.

"Parker's Back" is a story of a search for the roots of personal dissatisfaction. There are two epiphanies in the narrative (in Joyce's sense of moments of heightened consciousness), and along with these quiet realizations, there is a cataclysmic event that hurls the protagonist irrevocably into an altered awareness. The trauma in O. E. Parker's life is a farming accident: he absentmindedly drives a tractor into a huge tree, is hurled from the machine screaming "God above!" and watches as tractor, tree, and his own shoes burn. O'Connor tells us that "he could feel the hot breath of the burning tree on his face" as if the tree were animated with an intimate message, and that O. E. immediately careens away from the scene and heads toward the city in his truck. "Parker did not allow himself to think on the way to the city. He only knew that there had been a great change in his life, a leap into a worse unknown, and that there was nothing he could do about it." [24] The narration of this crisis is typical of O'Connor's handling of revelation. The character is passive, the experience is both unanticipated and unwanted. Something unspecified but disturbing has happened to his mind. But however much O. E. Parker may sense his own altered circumstances, his reaction is the programmed, mechanical solution that he has had for all of his internal anguish: he will get another tattoo.

The pattern of the narrative is, then, a pattern of obsession briefly but decisively interrupted. All of O. E.'s previous anxieties have been solved, at least temporarily, by getting a new tattoo. The colored images are each pleasing to O. E., and collectively they contribute to his goal of becoming like a tattoo artist he had seen as a boy. In flashback the reader is told that O. E. had seen the performer "flexing his muscles so that the arabesque of men and beasts and flowers on his skin appeared to have a subtle emotion, lifted up" (513). Of this first epiphany O'Connor tells us not only that he was moved but why. "Until he saw the man at the fair, it did not enter his head that there was anything out of the ordinary about the fact that he existed ... [it was] as if a blind boy had been turned so gently in a different direction that he did not know his destination had been changed" (513). In this instance, O'Connor makes full use of the omniscient voice, exposing both the subjective impression of the character and more than the character could possibly have divined (that the experience was in some way definitive). But the implications of this brief allusion to the change in Parker's life are obscure. For the "different direction" appears to be nothing more than a home cure; O. E. has acquired a remedy for his recurring dissatisfactions.

Just as the urge to engrave his body is irrational, so is Parker's marriage to a sallow religious fundamentalist. This woman, Sarah Ruth, questions Parker's tattooing impulse. "At the judgement seat of God, Jesus is going to say to you, 'What you been doing all your life besides have pictures drawn all over you?'" (519). She prefers him covered up or in the dark. It is a strange, strained union, initiated irrationally and continued irrationally; Parker especially is perplexed by his motivation for staying with such a woman.

Thus an obsession with tattoos and a preoccupation with pleasing a sour wife precede the trauma of Parker's accident, and these things shape his response to it. He will tattoo the image of Christ on his back, resolving his own anxiety about the accident in the accustomed manner and hoping also to please Sarah Ruth. After all, he reasons, "She can't say she don't like the looks of God" (525). To this point, this character's motivation is farfetched, improbable, but consistent. It is precisely at this point that O'Connor effects a radical change in his perception. The tattoo assumes an added significance to Parker, as if the psychic change that he had sought to effect with other pictures has finally been achieved. It is clear that the tattoo is not only a picture of Christ but an image with a keenly felt moral imperative. "Parker sat for a long time ... examining his soul. He saw it as a spider web of facts and lies that was not at all important to him but which appeared to be necessary in spite of his opinion. The eyes that were forever on his back were eyes to be obeyed. He was as certain of it as he had ever been of anything"

(527). This insight into the vanity of his previous life, the irrational identification of a tattoo with a command, is then shown to be identical to other unaccountable impulses. "Throughout his life, grumbling and sometimes cursing, often afraid, once in rapture, Parker had obeyed whatever instinct of this kind had come to him—in rapture when his spirit had lifted at the sight of the tattooed man at the fair, afraid when he had joined the navy, grumbling when he had married Sarah Ruth" (527). The second epiphany contains, then, the key to all of Parker's previous conduct; it reveals, as it were, a theme of the life, locating his feeling about the Christ tattoo in the larger context of his vulnerability toward the forces of irrationality. In the remaining narrative, Parker comes to terms with the implications of his new emotional allegiance, first by denying it in the face of his buddies' ridicule, then by identifying himself to his wife with his biblical name, Obadiah. The scene where Parker tries to gain entrance to his locked home, the scene where he acknowledges the new self by use of the new name, is rendered with the same hyperbolic dramatic machinery that had accompanied Mrs. Turpin's revelation. "The sky had lightened slightly and there were two or three streaks of yellow floating above the horizon. Then as he stood there, a tree of light burst over the skyline. Parker fell back against the door as if he had been pinned there by a lance" (528). The tree of light completes the insight begun by the burning tree in the farm accident; Parker recognizes himself as an Obadiah and, with this, receives the assurance that his choice is correct. At this moment, his "spider web soul turned into a perfect arabesque of colors, a garden of trees and birds and beasts" (528). The language echoes that used previously to describe the tattoo artist's exterior. Here, however, the condition described is an internal one; the language suggests metaphorically a lively harmony and, with it, a sense of peace, the implied end to a disgruntled quest. What had been sought as a condition of the body is received as a condition of the soul. The inversion is complete.

The story, however, is not completed with this reversal. Instead, O'Connor finishes the action in terms of Parker and Sarah Ruth's marital relationship. The wife, good fundamentalist that she has always been, rejects the "face of God" on Parker's back. To her, as to everyone of that religious persuasion, any image of God is a metaphor to be used, if at all, to assist the imagination. For her it contains no moral imperative. She beats her husband, raising welts on his back and consequently on this image. Parker ends this episode of his life under one of the trees that has been so important to him, in tears.

If we can accept the harshness of Sarah Ruth's character, the extremity of Parker's obsessions, and O'Connor's idea of what marriage is like, the story has some vague psychological coherence. Parker cries because a gesture intended to soften a brittle wife has failed, and because the image of Christ that has enlisted his moral allegiance is thought by Sarah Ruth to be blasphemous. Literally, it is blasphemous, and if the text is read on the level of psychological realism, then it is the story of a terrible mistake. But the difficulty of seeing the tattoo as only a tattoo, the strain of finding even thin psychological motivation that is sound, suggests that there is more to the story than marital strife. In fact, the incongruity between the comic gesture to please Sarah Ruth and the weight of surrounding circumstances—the burning trees, the eerie light, the piercing eyes of the Byzantine Christ—compels the search for a more contrived meaning to these strange events. In the end, a very simple device seems to be at work: O'Connor illustrates a man "getting religion" by effecting the "getting" literally. Christ is under the skin of Parker's back by virtue of a tattooist's needles. However, the conduct that follows is more fittingly the behavior of a man who has had a spiritual encounter with Christ rather than merely a physical alteration. Beyond this behavioral clue, there have been the revelations, the author's explanations at strategic points, and the exposure of consciousness at others to tell the audience in no uncertain way that O. E. Parker has met his God.

To the extent that "Parker's Back" is a contrived, obvious story, it is also an uncomfortable one to read. The postures of the author become distorted as she strains to make the action credible and at the same time representative of religious experience. O'Connor realized the awkwardness of her stance. "It's not necessary to point out that the look of this fiction is going to be wild, that it is almost of necessity going to be violent and comic, because of the discrepancies that it seeks to combine."[25] But it is not to violence or comedy that the reader objects; rather it is to the sense of meaning being forced into the unwilling mold of unrelated events, of actions having to carry disproportionate moral weight. As soon as O'Connor's vision is made accessible through whatever means, it subjects itself to being judged. The problem of distance between an author and readers changes from a problem of cognition—whether the audience can recognize intended meanings—to the problem of consent. It is at this point that an unambiguous moral position in a work of art runs the risk of being rejected; a message offered at the expense of good craftsmanship can exceed the bounds of rhetorical manipulation that most dispassionate audiences are willing to accept.

A reason for the tendentious suggestion in "Parker's Back" has already been suggested. At the point of death, facing for herself the issue that had been of central concern to characters in her fiction, O'Connor must have wanted to make sure that people understood her. In her final hours, the risk of offending a hostile audience must have seemed small indeed.

IV

It seems appropriate to end, however, with a discussion, not of O'Connor's last story, but with one written in mid-career. She admitted that this tale, "The Artificial Nigger," was her favorite story.[26] Subject to none of the cumbersome manipulation of "Parker's Back," it tells the story of common events in the lives of ordinary people, and manages nonetheless to make the experience of grace apparent.

Undoubtedly, it is one of her most engaging narratives, and it works on the anagogical as well as the literal level. During a symposium at Vanderbilt University in 1957 she explained the title.

Well, I never had heard the phrase before, but my
mother was out trying to buy a cow, and she rode up
the country a-piece. She had the address of a man who
was supposed to have a cow for sale, but she couldn't
find it, so she stopped in a small town and asked the
countryman on the side of the road where the house
was, and he said, "Well, you go into this town and you
can't miss it 'cause it's the only house in town with a
artificial nigger in front of it." So I decided I would
have to find a story to fit that. A little lower level than
starting with the theme.[27]

So the story began with an image, and O'Connor's imagination
worked from this toward construction of a narrative that would reveal the importance of the black plaster lawn fixture. Her description of the starting point is very similar to Faulkner's explanation of
the beginning of *The Sound and the Fury*. "It began with a mental
picture. I didn't realize at the time it was symbolical. The picture
was of the muddy seat of a little girl's drawers in a pear tree, where
she could see through a window where her grandmother's funeral
was taking place and report what was happening to her brothers on
the ground below."[28] Faulkner went on to discuss the process by
which he recognized the implications of the picture of Caddy and
translated it into narrative. Of a similar procedure in O'Connor's
thinking, we have no record; but the mental route must have been
devious, for the story begins very far from the middle-class lawns
where such statuary is usually to be found in the South.

The story is simple in conception. Mr. Head, an old man bringing
up his only grandson alone, decides to take the boy to the city for
the first time. The trip, designed to teach "a lesson that the boy
would never forget," is a disaster, for Mr. Head gets lost and barely
succeeds in catching the last train home. The sojourn in the city is,
in effect, a descent into hell for both of them; they spend hours
bleakly confronting their own ignorance and, finally, their alienation from each other. In establishing the isolation and disgrace that
overcome these two, in portraying their loss of innocence, O'Con-

nor is masterful, for it is the depth of this domestic despair that measures the joyousness of their final reunion. Unlike many situations in the O'Connor canon, "The Artificial Nigger" ends with the release of tension and the reestablishment of trust.

The pivotal event in the story is Mr. Head's denial of Nelson. Young and eager to convince his grandfather of his independence, the boy had annoyed the old man with the reminder that he had been born in the city and that he was, in fact, returning to it. To Mr. Head, this is nonsense; he wants the boy to recognize the vanity of city life and, conversely, to understand his own will and strong character.

Although the old man does not realize it, this process begins almost as soon as the journey gets underway. There had been a long-standing dispute about whether the child would recognize a Negro if he saw one; he doesn't. Nelson moves to leave the train at the wrong station; Mr. Head corrects him. O'Connor tells her readers what the grandfather is too self-absorbed to recognize, that "for the first time in his life, he [Nelson] understood that his grandfather was indispensable to him."[29] With this comment, O'Connor lays the foundation for the dramatic irony that follows, for Mr. Head remains bent on proving what the readers already know to be unnecessary. Nelson's discomfort and recognition of dependence have begun before he sets foot in this unnamed city. What follows, then, as the old man tries to further the boy's education, is seen to be gratuitously cruel. At the boy's moments of greatest vulnerability, the old man deserts him: first, he hides when the boy wakes from an exhausted nap; then, when the child has upset a woman's groceries by his panicked response to solitude, Mr. Head denies his kinship: "This is not my boy . . . I never seen him before" (265).

In the remainder of the story, O'Connor leads her audience as Mr. Head had never been able to lead young Nelson. She indicates the spiritual dilemma of both man and boy in ways that would not have occurred to them, in language beyond their command. Nelson becomes a mute zombie, unreachable by the normal human gestures of reconciliation. Silent and disconsolate, he drags behind Mr. Head, who experiences increasingly the horror of his denial. The author enters the mind of her character, not only revealing but reformulating the emotions that surface therein. Mr. Head wants to fall into the sewers and be swept away in the disgusting elements that mirror his soul; he sees his future as a hollow tunnel; he knows that he is "wandering into a black strange place where nothing was like it had ever been before, a long old age without respect and an end that would be welcome because it would be the end" (267). This inner malaise is so relentlessly disclosed that when the old man calls to a fat suburbanite in bermuda shorts, "Oh Gawd, I'm lost!" (267), his cry expresses a despairing displacement of soul, even though the fat man responds, as he should, with directions to the nearest train station.

We are told, though, that physical relocation is not an answer, for the child has not recovered from his desertion; in a sense he has no home to return to. It is at this point that O'Connor intercedes, exposing the artificial nigger, the motivating image of her story, in a context that is heavy with latent emotion. The old man and boy stand amazed before this chipped piece of statuary, and O'Connor tells us exactly what they experience.

> They stood gazing at the artificial Negro as if they were faced with some great mystery, some monument to another's victory that brought them together in their common defeat. They could both feel it dissolving their differences like an action of mercy. Mr. Head had never known before what mercy felt like because he had been too good to deserve any, but he felt he knew now. He looked at Nelson and understood that he must say something to the child to show that he was still wise and in the look the boy returned he saw a hungry need for that assurance. Nelson's eyes seemed to implore him to explain once and for all the mystery of existence.

> Mr. Head opened his lips to make a lofty statement
> and heard himself say, "They ain't got enough real ones
> here. They got to have an artificial one." (264)

It is an object as strange to Nelson and Mr. Head as it was initially to
O'Connor that bridges the spiritual alienation of the man and boy.
There is no aura of portentous allusion surrounding the object;
it does not represent anything other than itself. But it functions
uniquely in the lives of the protagonists, enabling them to forgive
and be forgiven. In some ways, the scene is similar to the mental
encounters Franz Kafka described in his letters to Felice Bauer.
"For a long time now I have planned . . . to cut out and collect from
various papers news items that astonished me for some reason, that
affected me, that seemed . . . to be meant only for me." [30] In the same
way that the news items were public but of very particular, private
interest to Kafka, the statue is open for anyone to see; but it is especially important to Mr. Head and Nelson. To reinforce the sense
of releasing insight, O'Connor exposes Mr. Head's musings a second
time.

> Mr. Head stood very still and felt the action of mercy
> touch him again but this time he knew that there were
> no words in the world that could name it. He under-
> stood that it grew out of agony, which is not denied to
> any man and which is given in strange ways to chil-
> dren. He understood it was all a man could carry into
> death to give his Maker. . . . He stood appalled, judging
> himself with the thoroughness of God, while the action
> of mercy covered his pride like a flame and consumed
> it. (269)

The meaning of the encounter is unambiguously rendered. Nothing
is left hidden. With the disclosure of Mr. Head's thoughts, the author has revealed her own understanding as well. The reader is not
left to surmise an extraordinary significance for the statue, in
the way he was left to assign portentous meanings to the bull in
"Greenleaf." He is told straightforwardly that the statue has evoked

a religious experience and that Mr. Head's epiphany occurs in the terms of traditional Christian theology. It is the Christian God who has spoken to him, and the old man interprets his own character and situation in light of original sin, damnation, and release from suffering. O'Connor's willingness to assume the full privilege of omniscient author has carried her through this passage cleanly and without the heavy ambiguities that often linger in other scenes of supposed revelation. There is no room for a reader's misinterpretation here, for as so infrequently happens in O'Connor's work, nothing is left to inference.

I would suggest that in these times of moral relativity, at an historical moment when no communal values can guide the assignment of anagogical meanings in fiction, this is the most effective and ultimately the most graceful narrative approach for the writer of religious concern. For a statement of faith is easier for an agnostic reader to accept than O'Connor's usual tendency toward oblique insult, which ensues from the intimation that her fictional world is fraught with portentous meanings that we could see if only we were not such monstrous readers, and too limited to understand.

Conclusion: The Limits of Inference

To define the modern sensibility has always been an elusive goal, the project of cultural generalists in times when generalization seems least valuable. No list of attributes seems comprehensive or accurate, but perhaps this is as it should be. The concept of an attribute is, in essence, a concrete, positive one, whereas the sensibility of the modern seems to come closest to definition in terms of negations and doubts. We live by means of disillusionment, without constructive alternatives to what we can no longer believe. As Irving Howe has said, "We establish our authenticity by the questions we allow to torment us."[1]

Whether this posture of uncertainty is commendable is open to question. Some would see it as a basis for the truest acts of human courage. But there are others who, like Flannery O'Connor, would consider this dubiety as a mark of poverty. Who is ultimately right is unimportant here; it is enough to articulate a difference.

It is an important difference. Writing about the reception of medieval and renaissance allegory in current times, Angus Fletcher observed that "obscurity appears to be a price necessarily paid for the lack of a universal, common doctrinal background. If readers do not share this background with the author, they may still be impressed by the ornaments of the vision without the cosmic reference."[2] His observation is relevant to Flannery O'Connor's work as well, for current literature that makes a claim to ultimate certainty does so in a cultural climate more comfortably attuned to hesitancy; and the consequence of this discrepancy is the need to educate and to persuade.

O'Connor's persuasive techniques were various. Through the use of grotesquery she tried to imply its opposite—the "whole man" in the Christian sense. Through allusion and analogy, she attempted to establish a private topology, a series of biblical analogues to her contemporary prophets. She worked to convey judgments through the implicit perspective of the narrating voice, to dramatize the experience of revelation, and, on rare occasions, to address the reader with what was beyond dramatization. But in any word sequence, what is intended and what is understood do not always coincide.

It has been the concern of this volume to make explicit the ways in which texts are decoded, to indicate the procedures by which we infer meanings from the heightened rhetoric of narration. Interpretation is a constructive process, dependent to some extent on the nature of the perceiving mind; but a reader constructs according to identifiable qualities of language. These constitute the artist's evidence. For this reason, effective communication is dependent on two things: the author's anticipation of his readers' assumptions, and the execution of a fictional manipulation that will reach such an audience.

But consider this problem carefully. To some extent it is impossible to anticipate a hostile audience, to overcome in one's person "the lack of . . . common doctrinal background." "In the last analysis," O'Connor remarked with admirable insight, "the only reader [the artist] can know is himself." He can also be reasonably sure of other minds that are similarly trained, for communication occurs, again as O'Connor knew, within a community.[3] As numerous critics have attested, those who already belong to the Christian community are able to read this author on her own anagogical terms. But their readings have been guided both by O'Connor's comments on her work and by their own predisposition to see anagogically and so to fill in what is unstated in the text. Thus, they are doubly dependent on conditions outside the text for extending the evidence of the text beyond what is warranted. But what of the "monstrous reader," the reader outside that select community of believers? Wayne Booth has demonstrated that "any story will be unintelligible unless it includes, however subtly, the amount of telling necessary not only to make us aware of the value system which gives it its meaning, but, more importantly, to make us willing to accept that value system." [4]

For whatever reasons (and reasons of this kind must remain speculative), O'Connor was manifestly hesitant to "tell" enough to make textual meanings unambiguous to the nonreligious. Her problem was twofold. Not only did her readers not "get" the theological overtones—her methods of indirection often prohibited inferring the intended theological meaning of the fiction—but they did not "want it" either. In a sense, the agnostic reader might be compared to Sarah Ruth in "Parker's Back." Our intellectual conventions prohibit beating the individual of Christian persuasion, but the rejection would be there nonetheless. The Christian tattoo might have a moral imperative for O. E. Parker or Flannery O'Connor, but for such a reader, it would be "just a picture."

But for the moment, let us consider the work of art as just a picture. What *is* seen is of the greatest importance. Flannery O'Connor wanted to make her audience see in a certain extended sense; she thought of herself as a prophet. But it should be remembered that the writer wanted what she suspected might be impossible. Her fictional prophets went into the city only to discover their own singularity. Proselytizing called attention more to the isolation and vulnerability of the believer than to the receptiveness of the secular inhabitants. Old Tarwater lived in a wilderness with one dubious disciple. His nephew's fate was probably harder, since young Tarwater realized the implications of his calling at an earlier age and was faced with prophesying to a hostile and, for him, unmanageable city. There is a sad analogy in this with the life of the solitary, wry, intensely religious woman from Georgia who periodically sent her manuscripts up to New York City. The message was sent in writing; the missionary journey was undertaken in the metaphorical sense only, though, I conclude, with the same questionable effectiveness. But there is this distinction: in the crafting of language, O'Connor was masterful. She wrote, as she knew, because she was "good at it." She became, as she hoped she would, "self forgetful in order to meet the demands of the thing seen and the thing made."[5] The "thing made" often must have demanded rendering in terms of the secular characteristics of contemporary southern culture.

There are two reasons, then, that can account for O'Connor's lack of success as a writer of anagogical fiction. One is the writer's difficulty in second-guessing the perceptions of her secular readers and anticipating how much "telling" to incorporate in the text. The other is more positive, and can be identified with what Maritain has called "the habit of art."[6] It is involved with the artist's realization that the truth of rendering in art need not coincide with the truths of religion; for truth, in this sense, has more to do with beauty—an accuracy of selection and composition—than with moral precepts. It is important, then, to ask how much it matters that O'Connor's anagogy often remains inaccessible.

Throughout these stories there is commonly a quality of honesty, a consistent sharpness, the relief of humor, and an extended exposure of human weakness and pretension. With the agrarians of the 30s, O'Connor shared a desire to explode the myth of progress and the secular faith in human perfectibility. That Christian and agnostic can share common perceptual ground is a thought that probably would have made O'Connor uncomfortable. As an artist who saw in terms of salvation and damnation, she looked at most of the disciplines of human endeavor as partial and therefore evil. But even she realized that the Judeo-Christian tradition has formed the shape of our secularism.[7] One need not look at life from the perspective of eternity to laugh at weakness, to see that we repeatedly fall short of the better selves that we imagine. It need not matter that we frame our ideals in psychological, social, or political terms rather than the stringent ones of fundamentalist religion. For in either case, failure is our common end. To have framed these problems cogently in a vital southern idiom, to have represented the absurdity of mundane concerns and the precariousness of material well being, to have posed a threat to narrow and habitual points of view—these are Flannery O'Connor's achievements. And they are valuable even according to the terms in which she most wanted to be judged—those of Saint Thomas Aquinas.

In the letters she wrote to friends over the years, O'Connor frequently spoke of her goal as "the accurate naming of the things of God"; and then she explained that, like Conrad, she wanted "to render the highest possible justice to the visible universe."[8] This is, of course, also the language of Aquinas when he speaks of truth as "the congruence of thing and intellect," for naming can be thought of as the intellectualizing of things. To the extent that she called folly by its right name, she was a truth teller in both a doctrinally condoned and a more widely recognized sense. This is an accomplishment that remains unaffected by the limits of inference. Even when unembellished by revealed anagogical implications, Flannery O'Connor's work retains a weight of human concern that makes the reading of the fiction a disturbing encounter, valuable to readers of any persuasion because its haunting truth rests on sharable experience rather than prohibitive religious allusion.

Chronology of Flannery O'Connor's Fiction

The following list includes the publication in which O'Connor first published each piece, together with information about how the tales were collected or incorporated into the later novels.

1946   "The Geranium." *Accent* (Summer); later included in *The Complete Stories of Flannery O'Connor*.

1947   University of Iowa master's thesis, containing: "The Barber" (see 1970), "Wildcat" (see 1970), "The Crop" (see 1971), "The Turkey" (revised as "The Capture" [see 1948]), "The Geranium" (see 1946), and "The Train" (see 1948); all included in *The Complete Stories*.

1948   "The Train." *Sewanee Review* (April); revised as Chapter 1 of *Wise Blood*; Original version included in *The Complete Stories*.

"The Capture." *Mademoiselle* (November); a revision of "The Turkey" (see 1947).

1949   "The Heart of the Park." *Partisan Review* (February); revised as Chapter 5 of *Wise Blood*; included in *The Complete Stories*.

"The Woman on the Stairs." *Tomorrow* (August); revised as "A Stroke of Good Fortune" (see 1953).

"The Peeler." *Partisan Review* (December); revised as Chapter 3 of *Wise Blood*; included in *The Complete Stories*.

1952   "Enoch and the Gorilla." *New World Writing* I (April); revised for Chapters 11 and 12 of *Wise Blood*; included in *The Complete Stories*.
Wise Blood.

1953   "A Good Man is Hard to Find." *The Berkeley Book of Modern Writing* I (ed. William Phillips and Philip Rahv); included in *A Good Man Is Hard to Find* and *The Complete Stories*.
"The Life You Save May Be Your Own." *Kenyon Review* (Spring); included in *A Good Man Is Hard to Find* and *The Complete Stories*.
"A Stroke of Good Fortune." *Shenandoah* (Spring); included in *A Good Man Is Hard to Find* and *The Complete Stories*.
"The River." *Sewanee Review* (Summer); included in *A Good Man Is Hard to Find* and *The Complete Stories*.
"A Late Encounter with the Enemy." *Harper's Bazaar* (September); included in *A Good Man Is Hard to Find* and *The Complete Stories*.

1954   "A Circle in the Fire." *Kenyon Review* (Spring); included in *A Good Man Is Hard to Find* and *The Complete Stories*.
"A Temple of the Holy Ghost." *Harper's Bazaar* (May); included in *A Good Man Is Hard to Find* and *The Complete Stories*.
"The Displaced Person." *Sewanee Review* (October); enlarged and included in *A Good Man Is Hard to Find* and *The Complete Stories*.

1955   "The Artificial Nigger." *Kenyon Review* (Spring); included in *A Good Man Is Hard to Find* and *The Complete Stories*.
"Good Country People." *Harper's Bazaar* (June); included in *A Good Man Is Hard to Find* and *The Complete Stories*.

"You Can't Be Any Poorer Than Dead." *New World Writing* VIII (October); revised as Chapter 1 of *The Violent Bear it Away*.

A Good Man Is Hard to Find.

1956   "Greenleaf." *Kenyon Review* (Summer); included in *Everything That Rises Must Converge* and *The Complete Stories*.

1957   "A View of the Woods." *Partisan Review* (Fall); included in *Everything That Rises Must Converge* and *The Complete Stories*.

1958   "The Enduring Chill." *Harper's Bazaar* (July); included in *Everything That Rises Must Converge* and *The Complete Stories*.

1960   "The Comforts of Home." *Kenyon Review* (Fall); included in *Everything That Rises Must Converge* and *The Complete Stories*.

The Violent Bear It Away.

1961   "Everything That Rises Must Converge." *New World Writing* XVIII; included in *Everything That Rises Must Converge* and *The Complete Stories*.

"The Partridge Festival." *Critic* (February–March); included in *The Complete Stories*.

1962   "The Lame Shall Enter First." *Sewanee Review* (Summer); included in *Everything That Rises Must Converge* and *The Complete Stories*.

1963   "Why Do the Heathen Rage?" *Esquire* (July); beginning of unfinished third novel; included in *The Complete Stories*.

1964   "Revelation." *Sewanee Review* (Spring); included in *Everything That Rises Must Converge* and *The Complete Stories*.

1965   "Parker's Back." *Esquire* (April); included in *Everything That Rises Must Converge* and *The Complete Stories*.

"Judgement Day." Included in *Everything That Rises Must Converge* and *The Complete Stories*.

Everything That Rises Must Converge.

1970   "Wildcat." *North American Review* (Spring); included in *The Complete Stories.*
"The Barber." *Atlantic* (October); included in *The Complete Stories.*

1971   "The Crop." *Mademoiselle* (April); included in *The Complete Stories.*
The Complete Stories of Flannery O'Connor.

Notes

Introduction

1 E. A. R. Ennion and N. Tinbergen, *Tracks* (Oxford, England: Oxford University Press, 1967), 13. For calling my attention to this book, I am indebted to E. H. Gombrich, "The Evidence of Images," in C. S. Singleton (ed.), *Interpretation: Theory and Practice* (Baltimore: Johns Hopkins University Press, 1969), 35–104.

2 *Object* does not refer necessarily to something that exists in the world, for often the fiction imitates nothing that exists concretely. Thus the object of representation may refer to the imaginings of the author, to the contents of mind. For further discussion of this, see William H. Gass, *Fiction and the Figures of Life* (New York: Alfred A. Knopf, 1972), 37.

3 Morris R. Cohen and Ernest Nagel, *An Introduction to Logic* (New York: Harcourt, Brace and World, 1962), 7–8.

4 Flannery O'Connor to "A.," August 2, 1955, in Sally Fitzgerald (ed.), *The Habit of Being: Letters of Flannery O'Connor* (New York: Farrar, Straus, Giroux, 1979), 92.

5 David Eggenschwiler, *The Christian Humanism of Flannery O'Connor* (Detroit: Wayne State University Press, 1972), 13.

6 Flannery O'Connor, *Mystery and Manners: Occasional Prose*, ed. Sally and Robert Fitzgerald (New York: Farrar, Straus, Giroux, 1970), 47.

7 See Miles Orvell, *Invisible Parade: The Fiction of Flannery O'Connor* (Philadelphia: Temple University Press, 1972), 52.

8 Robert Fitzgerald, Introduction, *Everything That Rises Must Converge*, by Flannery O'Connor (New York: Farrar, Straus, Giroux, 1956), xvi.

9 For an attempt to construe the nature of O'Connor's personal beliefs from her readings in theology, see Sister Kathleen Feeley, *Flannery O'Connor: Voice of the Peacock* (New Brunswick: Rutgers University Press, 1972).

10 Josephine Hendin, *The World of Flannery O'Connor* (Bloomington: Indiana University Press, 1970), 7.

11 Richard Stern, "Flannery O'Connor: A Remembrance and Some Letters," *Shenandoah*, XVI (Winter, 1965), 5–6.

12 Hendin, *World of Flannery O'Connor*, 12–15.

13 Margaret I. Meaders, "Flannery O'Connor: 'Literary Witch,'" *Colorado Quarterly*, X (Spring, 1962), 385.

14 Betsy Lockridge, "An Afternoon with Flannery O'Connor," Atlanta *Journal and Constitution*, November 1, 1959, p. 40.

15 C. Ross Mullins, Jr., "Flannery O'Connor: An Interview," *Jubilee*, XI (June, 1963), 35.

16 O'Connor, *Mystery and Manners*, 224.

17 Flannery O'Connor, *A Good Man Is Hard to Find* (New York: Harcourt, Brace, 1955), 143.

18 See Victor Erlich, *Russian Formalism: History and Doctrine* (The Hague: Mouton, 1965), 178.

19 Although only seven of O'Connor's stories are discussed here, they can be taken as representative, given O'Connor's propensity to repeat narrative structures. Many of the stories were revised and published under separate titles, or incorporated in later novels. For example, "The Geranium," the opening story of O'Connor's master's thesis at the Iowa Writers Workshop, was rewritten and published posthumously in 1965 as "Judgement Day." The stories "The Train," "The Peeler," "The Heart of the Park," and "Enoch and the Gorilla" were all eventually incorporated into the novel *Wise Blood*. Similarly, "You Can't Be Any Poorer Than Dead" became the opening chapter of *The Violent Bear It Away*. Also, O'Connor inclined toward the same situations and character types even in stories that are quite dissimilar in superficial tenor. "The Lame Shall Enter First" repeats the situation of a dry intellectual getting his comeuppance from a young, "uncivilized" boy like the one in *The Violent Bear It Away*. "The Comforts of Home" and "The Enduring Chill" reiterate the dependent child-widowed mother relationship of "Greenleaf." In "The Temple of the Holy Ghost," there is a child as sour and ugly as the one in "The Circle in the Fire."

20 Irving Howe, "On Flannery O'Connor," *New York Review of Books* (September 30, 1965), 16. "Flannery O'Connor could bring into play resources of worldliness such as one might find in the work of a good many sophisticated modern writers. . . . Except for an occasional phrase, which serves partly as a rhetorical signal that more than ordinary verisimilitude is at stake, there are no unavoidable pressures to consider these stories in a strictly religious sense. They stand securely on their own, as

renderings and criticisms of human experience." See also, John Hawkes, "Flannery O'Connor's Devil," *Sewanee Review*, LXX (Summer, 1962), 398.

One

1 Robert Fitzgerald, Introduction, *Everything That Rises Must Converge*, by Flannery O'Connor (New York: Farrar, Straus, Giroux, 1956), xxxiii.

2 Flannery O'Connor, *Mystery and Manners: Occasional Prose*, ed. Sally and Robert Fitzgerald (New York: Farrar, Straus, Giroux, 1970), 32. "I see from the standpoint of Christian orthodoxy. This means that for me the meaning of life is centered in our Redemption by Christ and what I see in the world, I see in its relation to that."

3 Wilfrid Sheed, "The Good Word: On Keeping Closets Closed," *New York Times Book Review* (September 2, 1973), 2.

4 Erich Auerbach, *Mimesis: The Representation of Reality in Western Literature* (Princeton: Princeton University Press, 1953).

5 Joseph Conrad, quoted in O'Connor, *Mystery and Manners*, 80.

6 Flannery O'Connor to "A.," July 5, 1958, in Sally Fitzgerald (ed.), *The Habit of Being: Letters of Flannery O'Connor* (New York: Farrar, Straus, Giroux, 1979), 290.

7 O'Connor, *Mystery and Manners*, 15.

8 Northrop Frye, *Anatomy of Criticism* (Princeton: Princeton University Press, 1957), 136.

9 *The Fragments of the Works of Heraclitus of Ephesus*, trans. G. T. W. Patrick (Baltimore: University of Maryland Press, 1889), 86.

10 The history and complexity of biblical exegesis is too broad to be discussed here. It is not the purpose of this essay to make fine distinctions about the methods of interpreting the Scriptures, but to make a general statement about the difference between the experience of reading the Bible and reading a piece of prose fiction. For additional comment on exegesis, see C. M. Laymon (ed.), *The Interpreter's One Volume Commentary on the Bible* (New York: Abingdon, 1971), 947.

11 Flannery O'Connor, "The Fiction Writer and His Country," in Granville Hicks (ed.), *The Living Novel: A Symposium* (New York: Macmillan, 1957); Leon V. Driskell and Joan T. Brittain, *The Eternal Crossroads: The Art of Flannery O'Connor* (Lexington: University of Kentucky Press, 1971), 10. "Time's reviewer of *A Good Man Is Hard to Find* did not recognize that Miss O'Connor's gaze extended to the mysterious realm 'which is the concern of prophets,' for the review speaks of 'ten witheringly sarcastic stories' set in a South that moves along a 'sort of up-to-date Tobacco Road paved right into town.' This reading represents the early majority view; as Sister Bertrande writes in 'Esprit's' memorial issue to Miss O'Connor, real understanding of her work awaited the appearance of Miss O'Connor's essay, 'The Fiction Writer and His Country,' in Gran-

ville Hicks's *The Living Novel.*" See also Caroline Gordon, "Heresy in Dixie," *Sewanee Review*, LXXVI (Spring, 1968), 267.

12 O'Connor to Sally and Robert Fitzgerald, May 8, 1955, 82, O'Connor to "A.," July 20, 1955, 90, and September 30, 1955, 108, all in Sally Fitzgerald (ed.), *The Habit of Being.*

13 John Hawkes, "Flannery O'Connor's Devil," *Sewanee Review*, LXX (Summer, 1962), 395–407; Nathan A. Scott, Jr., *The Broken Center: Studies in the Theological Horizon of Modern Literature* (New Haven: Yale University Press, 1966); Driskell and Brittain, *The Eternal Crossroads*, 10. When O'Connor was asked to write an introductory note for the second edition of *Wise Blood*, she explicitly directed attention to what had gone unnoticed—the theological issue of free will.

14 David Eggenschwiler, *The Christian Humanism of Flannery O'Connor* (Detroit: Wayne State University Press, 1972), 13.

15 Carter W. Martin, *The True Country: Themes in the Fiction of Flannery O'Connor* (Nashville: Vanderbilt University Press, 1968), 9.

16 Sister Kathleen Feeley, *Flannery O'Connor: Voice of the Peacock* (New Brunswick: Rutgers University Press, 1972), 14.

17 W. K. Wimsatt, *The Verbal Icon* (New York: Farrar, Straus and Cudahy, 1954), 3–18; O'Connor, *Mystery and Manners*, 126.

18 O'Connor to "A.," Wednesday [December, 1959], in Sally Fitzgerald (ed.), *The Habit of Being*, 362.

19 This is one of the essential questions raised by the study of O'Connor's work, but it has rarely been seen as a problem. Instead of critical inquiry, past scholarship has been filled with assertions. For example, see Martin, *The True Country*, 11. The source of his observations is not the examination of language, but biography. Because there is clear evidence that O'Connor read Mircea Eliade's book, *The Sacred and the Profane* (see Feeley, *Flannery O'Connor*, 115), it has been assumed that Eliade's concept of "hierophany" effectively shaped her fiction. While his concept of the potential extensions of meaning in the physical environment adequately accounts for the nature of Martin's critical remarks, it does not account for O'Connor's fiction. For critics to predicate their judgments of prose on the substance of O'Connor's reading, however much she may have agreed with what she read, is to assume what should be proved. The "sacramental view" must be discoverable from the text itself.

20 Jan Schreiber, "The Poetry of Statement" (Ph.D dissertation, Brandeis University, 1972), 15.

21 T. S. Eliot, *The Complete Poems and Plays* (New York: Harcourt Brace and World, 1962), 38.

22 The arguments of E. D. Hirsch, *Validity in Interpretation* (New Haven: Yale University Press, 1967) have influenced the shape of my analysis. See especially Chap. 2.

23 See Schreiber, "The Poetry of Statement," for discussion of other textual situations.

24 Martin, *The True Country*, 11. See also O'Connor, *Mystery and Manners*, 157, 175 ("The artist penetrates the concrete world in order to find at its depths the image of its source, the image of ultimate reality").

25 Wallace Stevens, *Collected Poems* (New York: Knopf, 1967), 528.

26 O'Connor, *Mystery and Manners*, 168.

27 *Ibid.*, 180.

Two

1 Jean Stein, "William Faulkner, An Interview," in F. J. Hoffman and O. W. Vickery (eds.), *William Faulkner: Three Decades of Criticism* (New York: Harcourt, Brace and World, 1960), 76.

2 Henry James, *Hawthorne* (Ithaca: Cornell University Press, 1956). The whole book constitutes a critique of Hawthorne's relation to the American environment. See especially p. 11.

3 John Brooks, "Some Notes on Writing One Kind of Novel," in Granville Hicks (ed.), *The Living Novel: A Symposium* (New York: Macmillan, 1957), 41.

4 Flannery O'Connor, *Mystery and Manners: Occasional Prose*, ed. Sally and Robert Fitzgerald (New York: Farrar, Straus, Giroux, 1970), 32.

5 Virginia Woolf, "Modern Fiction," *The Common Reader* (London: The Hogarth Press, 1925), 153.

6 Flannery O'Connor to "A.," December 9, 1961, in Sally Fitzgerald (ed.), *The Habit of Being: Letters of Flannery O'Connor* (New York: Farrar, Straus, Giroux, 1979), 458.

7 O'Connor, *Mystery and Manners*.

8 *Ibid.*, 195–96.

9 *Ibid.*, 171.

10 J. E. Flower, *Intention and Achievement: An Essay on the Novels of Francois Mauriac* (Oxford: Clarendon Press, 1969), 16, 233.

11 Philip Stratford, *Faith and Fiction: Creative Process in Greene and Mauriac* (Notre Dame: University of Notre Dame Press, 1964), 202.

12 Flower, *Intention and Achievement*, 25.

13 A. A. Devitis, "The Catholic as Novelist: Graham Greene and Francois Mauriac," in R. O. Evans (ed.), *Graham Greene* (Lexington: University of Kentucky Press, 1967), 118.

14 Stratford, *Faith and Fiction*, 327.

15 Flower, *Intention and Achievement*, 26–28.

16 Devitis, "The Catholic as Novelist," 115.

17 Graham Greene, "Why I Write," in Evans (ed.), *Graham Greene*, 220.

18 O'Connor, *Mystery and Manners*, 176, 81.

19 Flower, *Intention and Achievement*, 95.

20 O'Connor, *Mystery and Manners*, 171.

21 Sister Kathleen Feeley, *Flannery O'Connor: Voice of the Peacock* (New Brunswick: Rutgers University Press, 1972), 19–20.

22 O'Connor, *Mystery and Manners*, 196.

23 *Ibid.*, 172.

24 Feeley, *Flannery O'Connor*, 45.

25 O'Connor, *Mystery and Manners*, 161, 185.

26 *Ibid.*, 166.

27 *Ibid.*, 124.

28 John Ruskin, *The Complete Works of John Ruskin*, ed. G. T. Cook and A. Wedderburn (London: George Allen, 1904), XI, 251–54.

29 Herman Melville, *Pierre, or the Ambiguities* (New York: New American Library, 1957), 476.

30 Leon V. Driskell and Joan T. Brittain, *The Eternal Crossroads: The Art of Flannery O'Connor* (Lexington: University of Kentucky Press, 1971), 25.

31 Flannery O'Connor, "The Novelist and Free Will," *Fresco*, I (Winter, 1961), 100–101.

32 For a cogent discussion of realism in narrative fiction, see René Wellek and Austin Warren, *Theory of Literature* (New York: Harcourt, Brace and World, 1956), 213.

33 O'Connor, *Mystery and Manners*, 33–34.

34 Walter Sullivan, *Death by Melancholy: Essays on Modern Southern Fiction* (Baton Rouge: Louisiana State University Press, 1972), 33.

35 O'Connor, *Mystery and Manners*, 33.

36 *Ibid.*, 96.

37 Ruth Vande Kieft, "Judgment in the Fiction of Flannery O'Connor," *Sewanee Review*, LXXVI (Spring, 1968), 356.

38 Flannery O'Connor to Sister Mariella Gable, May 4, 1963, in Carter W. Martin, *The True Country* (Nashville: Vanderbilt University Press, 1968), 14.

39 O'Connor, *Mystery and Manners*, 50, 41.

Three

1 Sister Kathleen Feeley, *Flannery O'Connor: Voice of the Peacock* (New Brunswick: Rutgers University Press, 1972), 8.

2 For similar responses, see *ibid.*, 18.

3 Wolfgang Kayser, *The Grotesque in Art and Literature*, trans. Ulrich Weisstein (New York: McGraw Hill, 1963), 185; William V. O'Connor, *The Grotesque: An American Genre and Other Essays* (Carbondale: Southern Illinois University Press, 1962), 4; Nathan A. Scott, Jr., *The Broken Center: Studies in the Theological Horizon of Modern Literature* (New Haven: Yale University Press, 1966), 21.

4 Flannery O'Connor, *Mystery and Manners: Occasional Prose*, ed. Sally and Robert Fitzgerald (New York: Farrar, Straus, Giroux, 1970), 168, 44.

5 Feeley, *Flannery O'Connor*, 24, 29.

6 O'Connor, *Mystery and Manners*, 177.

7 William Butler Yeats, *The Autobiography of William Butler Yeats* (New York: Macmillan, 1965), 25.

8 O'Connor, *Mystery and Manners*, 177–78. See Jan Schreiber, "Crucifixus," *Southern Review*, XI (1975), 860, for an alternate point of view.

9 O'Connor, *Mystery and Manners*, 109.

10 Flannery O'Connor, "Good Country People," in *The Complete Stories of Flannery O'Connor*, ed. Sally Fitzgerald (New York: Farrar, Straus, Giroux, 1971), 288. All subsequent references to this story will be indicated by page number in the text.

11 O'Connor, *Mystery and Manners*, 99.

12 Flannery O'Connor to James Farnham, undated, in Gilbert H. Muller, *Nightmares and Visions* (Athens: University of Georgia Press, 1972), 21.

13 O'Connor, *Mystery and Manners*, 40.

14 Gerald E. Sherry, "An Interview with Flannery O'Connor," *Critic*, XXI (June–July, 1963), 29.

15 O'Connor, *Mystery and Manners*, 133.

16 O'Connor, "A Circle in the Fire," in *The Complete Stories of Flannery O'Connor*, 175. All subsequent references to this story will be indicated by page number in the text.

17 Daniel 3.

18 For support of this reading, see Feeley, *Flannery O'Connor*, 185.

19 Sherwood Anderson, *Winesburg, Ohio* (New York: Viking Press, 1960), 24.

20 O'Connor, *Mystery and Manners*, 204.

Four

1 Flannery O'Connor, *Mystery and Manners: Occasional Prose*, ed. Sally and Robert Fitzgerald (New York: Farrar, Straus, Giroux, 1970), 112.

2 Yvor Winters, *Forms of Discovery* (Chicago: Swallow Press, 1967), xiii.

3 Flannery O'Connor, "The Novelist and Free Will," *Fresco* (Winter, 1961), 100–101.

4 O'Connor, *Mystery and Manners*, 98–99, 68.

5 René Wellek and Austin Warren, *Theory of Literature* (New York: Harcourt, Brace and World, 1956), 186–211.

6 Robert Fitzgerald, Introduction, *Everything That Rises*

Must Converge, by Flannery O'Connor (New York: Farrar, Straus, Giroux, 1956), xi.

7 See, for example, Miles Orvell, *Invisible Parade: The Fiction of Flannery O'Connor* (Philadelphia: Temple University Press, 1972), 31–39. See also Flannery O'Connor's own comments in *Mystery and Manners*, 39.

8 Mary McCarthy, "Settling the Colonel's Hash," in L. S. Hall (ed.), *A Grammar of Literary Criticism* (New York: Macmillan, 1965), 344.

9 *Ibid.*

10 Flannery O'Connor, quoted in Sister Kathleen Feeley, *Flannery O'Connor: Voice of the Peacock* (New Brunswick: Rutgers University Press, 1972), 52.

11 Herman Melville, *Moby Dick* (New York: New American Library, 1961), 214.

12 F. O. Matthiessen, *American Renaissance: Art and Expression in the Age of Emerson and Whitman* (New York: Oxford University Press, 1968), 130.

13 The terms *phoros* and *theme* are taken from C. Perelman and L. Olbrechs, *The New Rhetoric* (Notre Dame: University of Notre Dame Press, 1969), 372, 381.

14 Philip Wheelwright, *Metaphor and Reality* (Bloomington: Indiana University Press, 1962), 155–56.

15 Perelman and Olbrechs, *The New Rhetoric*, 391.

16 Flannery O'Connor, "The Lame Shall Enter First," "The River," and "The Enduring Chill," in *The Complete Stories of Flannery O'Connor*, ed. Sally Fitzgerald (New York: Farrar, Straus, Giroux, 1971), 450, 162, 372.

17 A possible exception to this statement is the story "A Temple of the Holy Ghost," in *ibid.*, 236–48.

18 O'Connor, "Greenleaf," in *ibid.*, 333. All subsequent references to this story will be indicated by page number in the text.

19 McCarthy, "Settling the Colonel's Hash," 346.

20 Feeley, *Flannery O'Connor*, 95.

21 Orvell, *Invisible Parade*, 23.

22 *Ibid.*, 38.

23 Northrop Frye, *Anatomy of Criticism* (Princeton: Princeton University Press, 1957), 126.

24 Feeley, *Flannery O'Connor*, 172–76; see also C. W. Martin, *The True Country: Themes in the Fiction of Flannery O'Connor* (Nashville: Vanderbilt University Press, 1968), 94–104.

25 O'Connor, "The Displaced Person," in *The Complete Stories*, 214. All subsequent references to this story will be indicated by page number in the text.

26 Robert Fitzgerald, "The Countryside and the True Coun-

try," in Robert E. Reiter (ed.), *Flannery O'Connor, Christian Critics Series* (St. Louis: Herder, 1968), 78–79.

27 O'Connor, *Mystery and Manners*, 95–96.

28 See discussion of displacement in Chapter One.

29 Flannery O'Connor to "A.," July 20, 1955, in Sally Fitzgerald (ed.), *The Habit of Being: Letters of Flannery O'Connor* (New York: Farrar, Straus, Giroux, 1979), 90.

30 Feeley, *Flannery O'Connor*, 115.

Five

1 Flannery O'Connor, *The Violent Bear It Away* (New York: Farrar, Straus, Giroux, 1960), 242–43. All subsequent references to this novel will be indicated by page number in the text.

2 Stuart L. Burns, "Flannery O'Connor's *The Violent Bear It Away*: Apotheosis in Failure," *Sewanee Review*, LXXVI (Spring, 1968), 334; Clinton W. Trowbridge, "The Symbolic Vision of Flannery O'Connor: Patterns of Imagery in *The Violent Bear It Away*," *Sewanee Review*, LXXVI (Spring, 1968), 313.

3 Flannery O'Connor, *Mystery and Manners: Occasional Prose*, ed. Sally and Robert Fitzgerald (New York: Farrar, Straus, Giroux, 1970), 116.

4 Sister Kathleen Feeley, *Flannery O'Connor: Voice of the Peacock* (New Brunswick: Rutgers University Press, 1972), 54–55.

5 J. V. Cunningham, *Tradition and Poetic Structure* (Denver: Swallow Press, 1960), 269.

6 For a further explanation of the reader's dilemma, see Martha Stephens, *The Question of Flannery O'Connor* (Baton Rouge: Louisiana State University Press, 1973), 38.

7 Wayne C. Booth, *The Rhetoric of Fiction* (Chicago: University of Chicago Press, 1961), 289. "We must experience confusion, we must taste genuine ambiguity if its resolution is to seem either convincing or worthwhile."

8 Flannery O'Connor to Catharine Carver, April 18, 1959, in Sally Fitzgerald (ed.), *The Habit of Being: Letters of Flannery O'Connor* (New York: Farrar, Straus, Giroux, 1979), 327.

9 Booth, *Rhetoric of Fiction*, 243–66.

10 See the discussion of the same problem in Bruno Snell, *The Discovery of the Mind* (Cambridge: Harvard University Press, 1953), 19.

11 Feeley, *Flannery O'Connor*, 165.

12 Erich Auerbach, *Mimesis: The Representation of Reality in Western Literature*, trans. W. R. Trask (Princeton: Princeton University Press, 1968), 15.

13 Homer, *The Odyssey*, trans. E. V. Rieu (New York: Penguin, 1954), 10; Jane Austen, *Emma* (Boston: Houghton Mifflin, 1957), 1.

14 José Ortega y Gasset, *The Dehumanization of Art and Other Writings on Art and Culture*, trans. W. R. Trask (Garden City: Doubleday, 1956).

15 Matthew 14:14–21.

16 See, for example, Sister Jeremy, *"The Violent Bear It Away*: A Linguistic Education," *Renascence*, XVII (Fall, 1964), 11–16. Also, Robert McCown, "The Education of a Prophet: A Study of Flannery O'Connor's *The Violent Bear It Away*," *Kansas Magazine* (1962), 73–78, as well as Trowbridge, "The Symbolic Vision," and Burns, "Flannery O'Connor's *The Violent Bear It Away*."

17 O'Connor to "A.," July 25, 1959, in Sally Fitzgerald (ed.), *The Habit of Being*, 342.

18 Ruth Vande Kieft, "Judgment in the Fiction of Flannery O'Connor," *Sewanee Review*, LXXVI (Spring, 1968), 352.

19 C. Ross Mullins, Jr., "Flannery O'Connor: An Interview," *Jubilee*, XI (June, 1963), 35.

20 Josephine Hendin, *The World of Flannery O'Connor* (Bloomington: Indiana University Press, 1970), 10.

21 Burns, "Flannery O'Connor's *The Violent Bear It Away*," 336.

22 O'Connor to "A.," September 6, 1955, in Sally Fitzgerald (ed.), *The Habit of Being*, 100.

23 For a fuller explanation of this phrase, see David L. Rubin, "Toward a New View of Malherbe: Higher, Hidden Order in the First Completed Ode," *Papers of the Midwest Modern Language Association*, I (1969), 94–102.

Six

1 Lionel Trilling, Introduction, *The Collected Stories of Isaac Babel* (New York: Harcourt, Brace and World, 1960), 15.

2 Flannery O'Connor, *Mystery and Manners: Occasional Prose*, ed. Sally and Robert Fitzgerald (New York: Farrar, Straus, Giroux, 1970), 34.

3 Martha Stephens, *The Question of Flannery O'Connor* (Baton Rouge: Louisiana State University Press, 1973), 98.

4 Graham Greene, *Brighton Rock* (New York: Viking, 1956), 124.

5 Morris Beja, *Epiphany in the Modern Novel* (Seattle: University of Washington Press, 1971), 114.

6 *Ibid.*, 15.

7 James Joyce, *Stephen Hero* (New York: New Directions, 1969), 143.

8 *Ibid.*, 176.

9 James Joyce, *Portrait of the Artist* (New York: Viking, 1955), 221.

10 Acts 9.

11 James Joyce, *Dubliners* (New York: Viking, 1962), 35.

12 Virginia Woolf, *To the Lighthouse* (New York: Harcourt, Brace and World, 1955), 309–10, 249.

13 Marcel Proust, *Swann's Way* (New York: Modern Library, 1959), 78.

14 Flannery O'Connor, *Wise Blood* (New York: Farrar, Straus, Giroux, 1962).

15 Flannery O'Connor, "Greenleaf," in *The Complete Stories of Flannery O'Connor*, ed. Sally Fitzgerald (New York: Farrar, Straus, Giroux, 1971), 329.

16 O'Connor, "The River," in *ibid.*, 174.

17 Jan Schreiber, "The Poetry of Statement" (Ph.D. dissertation, Brandeis University, 1972), 107.

18 James Guetti, *The Limits of Metaphor: A Study of Melville, Conrad, and Faulkner* (Ithaca: Cornell University Press, 1967), 110.

19 O'Connor, *Wise Blood*, 74.

20 See discussion of *The Violent Bear It Away*, Chapter Five.

21 Miles Orvell, *Invisible Parade: The Fiction of Flannery O'Connor* (Philadelphia: Temple University Press, 1972), 39.

22 O'Connor, "Revelation," in *The Complete Stories*, 500. All subsequent references to this story will be indicated by page number in the text.

23 Sister Kathleen Feeley, *Flannery O'Connor: Voice of the Peacock* (New Brunswick: Rutgers University Press, 1972), 150.

24 O'Connor, "Parker's Back," in *The Complete Stories*, 521. All subsequent references to this story will be indicated by page number in the text.

25 O'Connor, *Mystery and Manners*, 43.

26 Katherine Fugin, "An Interview with Flannery O'Connor," *Censer* (Fall, 1960), 55.

27 Gilbert H. Muller, "The City of Woe: Flannery O'Connor's Dantean Vision," *Georgia Review*, XXIII (Summer, 1969), 206.

28 Jean Stein, "William Faulkner: An Interview," in F. J. Hoffman and O. W. Vickery (eds.), *William Faulkner: Three Decades of Criticism* (New York: Harcourt, Brace and World, 1960), 73.

29 O'Connor, "The Artificial Nigger," in *The Complete Stories*, 257. All subsequent references to this story will be indicated by page number in the text.

30 Franz Kafka, *Letters to Felice* (New York: Schocken, 1974), 61.

Conclusion

1 Irving Howe, *Decline of the New* (New York: Harcourt, Brace and World, 1970), 21.

2 E. H. Gombrich, "The Evidence of Images," in C. S. Singleton (ed.), *Interpretation: Theory and Practice* (Baltimore: Johns Hopkins University Press, 1969), 67.

3 Flannery O'Connor, *Mystery and Manners: Occasional Prose*, ed. Sally and Robert Fitzgerald (New York: Farrar, Straus, Giroux, 1970), 95, 53.

4 Wayne Booth, *The Rhetoric of Fiction* (Chicago: University of Chicago Press, 1961), 112.

5 O'Connor, *Mystery and Manners*, 82.

6 *Ibid.*, 101.

7 *Ibid.*, 155.

8 Flannery O'Connor to "A.," January 13, 1956, in Sally Fitzgerald (ed.), *The Habit of Being: Letters of Flannery O'Connor* (New York: Farrar, Straus, Giroux, 1979), 128.

Selected
Bibliography

Auden, W. H. "Postscript: Christianity and Art." *The Dyer's Hand and Other Essays*. New York: Random House, 1962.

Auerbach, Erich. *Mimesis: The Representation of Reality in Western Literature*. Translated by W. R. Trask. Princeton: Princeton University Press, 1953.

Ayer, Alfred J. *Language, Truth and Logic*. New York: Dover Publications, 1935.

Bassan, Maurice. "Flannery O'Connor's Way: Shock, with Moral Intent." *Renascence*, XV (Summer, 1963), 195–211.

Baumbach, Jonathan. *The Landscape of Nightmare*. New York: New York University Press, 1965.

Beardsley, M. C. *Aesthetics*. New York: Harcourt, Brace and World, 1958.

———. "Textual Meaning and Authorial Meanings." *Genre* (1968), 404–15.

Beja, Morris. *Epiphany in the Modern Novel*. Seattle: University of Washington Press, 1971.

Bellow, Saul. "The Writer and the Audience." *Perspectives*, IX (Autumn, 1954), 99–102.

Booth, Wayne C. *The Rhetoric of Fiction*. Chicago: University of Chicago Press, 1961.

Bowen, Robert O. "Hope versus Despair in the Gothic Novel." *Renascence*, XIII (Spring, 1961), 147–52.

Brooks, Cleanth. *The Hidden God: Studies in Hemingway, Faulkner, Yeats, Eliot, and Warren*. New Haven: Yale University Press, 1963.

Brooks, John. "Some Notes on Writing One Kind of Novel." In *The Living Novel: A Symposium*, edited by Granville Hicks. New York: Macmillan, 1957.

Burns, Stuart L. "Flannery O'Connor's *The Violent Bear It Away*: Apotheosis in Failure." *Sewanee Review*, LXXVI (Spring, 1968), 319–36.

Chase, Richard. *The American Novel and Its Tradition*. Garden City: Doubleday, 1957.

Cohen, Morris R., and Ernest Nagel. *An Introduction to Logic*. New York: Harcourt, Brace and World, 1962.

Corbett, E. P., ed. *Rhetorical Analyses of Literary Texts*. New York: Oxford University Press, 1969.

Crane, R. S. *The Languages of Criticism and the Structure of Poetry*. Toronto: University of Toronto Press, 1953.

Cunningham, J. V. *Tradition and Poetic Structure*. Denver: Alan Swallow, 1960.

————. *The Problem of Style*. Greenwich: Fawcett Publications, 1966.

Davidson, D. *Southern Writers in the Modern World*. Athens: University of Georgia Press, 1957.

Davis, B. "Flannery O'Connor: Christian Belief in Recent Fiction." *Listening* (Autumn, 1965), 5–21.

DeMan, Paul. "The Rhetoric of Temporality." In *Interpretation: Theory and Practice*, edited by C. S. Singleton. Baltimore: Johns Hopkins University Press, 1969.

Devitis, A. A. "The Catholic as Novelist: Graham Greene and Francois Mauriac." In *Graham Greene*, edited by R. O. Evans. Lexington: University of Kentucky Press, 1963.

Dowell, R. "The Moment of Grace in the Fiction of Flannery O'Connor." *College English*, VII (December, 1965), 235–39.

Drake, Robert. *Flannery O'Connor*. Contemporary Writers in Christian Perspective Series. Grand Rapids: William B. Eerdmans, 1966.

Driskell, Leon V., and Joan T. Brittain. *The Eternal Crossroads: The*

Art of Flannery O'Connor. Lexington: University of Kentucky Press, 1971.

Eggenschwiler, David. *The Christian Humanism of Flannery O'Connor*. Detroit: Wayne State University Press, 1972.

Empson, William. *Seven Types of Ambiguity*. New York: New Directions, 1947.

Enkvist, N. E., J. Spencer, and M. J. Gregory. *Linguistics and Style*. London: Oxford University Press, 1964.

Erlich, Victor. *Russian Formalism: History and Doctrine*. The Hague: Mouton, 1965.

Esprit. Flannery O'Connor memorial issue. VIII (Winter, 1964).

Esty, William. "The Gratuitous Grotesque." *Commonweal*, LXVII (March, 1958), 586–88.

Evans, R. O., ed. *Graham Greene*. Lexington: University of Kentucky Press, 1963.

Farnham, J. F. "The Grotesque in Flannery O'Connor." *America*, CV (May, 1961), 277.

Feeley, Sister Kathleen. *Flannery O'Connor: Voice of the Peacock*. New Brunswick: Rutgers University Press, 1972.

Feidelson, Charles, Jr. *Symbolism and American Literature*. Chicago: University of Chicago Press, 1953.

Fitzgerald, Robert. "The Countryside and The True Country." *Sewanee Review*, LXX (Summer, 1962), 380–94.

———. Introduction to *Everything That Rises Must Converge*, by Flannery O'Connor. New York: Farrar, Straus, Giroux, 1965.

Fletcher, Angus. *Allegory: The Theory of a Symbolic Mode*. Ithaca: Cornell University Press, 1964.

Flower, J. E. *Intention and Achievement: An Essay on the Novels of Francois Mauriac*. Oxford: Clarendon Press, 1969.

Friedman, M. J. *The Vision Obscured: Perceptions of Some Twentieth-Century Catholic Novelists*. New York: Fordham University Press, 1970.

Friedman, Melvin, and Lewis Lawson, eds. *The Added Dimension: The Art and Mind of Flannery O'Connor*. Rev. ed. New York: Fordham University Press, 1977.

Frye, Northrop. *Anatomy of Criticism*. Princeton: Princeton University Press, 1957.

Gable, Sister Mariella. *"Everything That Rises Must Converge."* *Critic*, XXIII (June–July, 1965), 58.

Gass, William. *Fiction and the Figures of Life*. New York: Alfred A. Knopf, 1971.

Gombrich, E. H. "The Evidence of Images." In *Interpretation: Theory and Practice*, edited by C. S. Singleton. Baltimore: Johns Hopkins University Press, 1969.

Gordon, Caroline. "Heresy in Dixie." *Sewanee Review*, LXXVI (Spring, 1968), 263–97.

Gossett, Louise Y. *Violence in Recent Southern Fiction*. Durham: Duke University Press, 1965.

Guetti, James. *The Limits of Metaphor: A Study of Melville, Conrad, and Faulkner*. Ithaca: Cornell University Press, 1967.

Halverson, M., and A. A. Cohen, eds. *A Handbook of Christian Theology*. Cleveland: World, Living Age, 1958.

Hawkes, John. "Flannery O'Connor's Devil." *Sewanee Review*, LXX (Summer, 1962), 395–407.

Hendin, Josephine. *The World of Flannery O'Connor*. Bloomington: Indiana University Press, 1970.

Hicks, Granville. "A Writer at Home with Her Heritage." *Saturday Review*, XLV (May, 1962), 22–23.

————, ed. *The Living Novel: A Symposium*. New York: Macmillan, 1957.

Hirsch, E. D. *Validity in Interpretation*. New Haven: Yale University Press, 1967.

Holman, C. Hugh. *The Roots of Southern Writing*. Athens: University of Georgia Press, 1972.

————. *Three Modes of Modern Southern Fiction*. Mercer University Lamar Series, No. 9. Athens: University of Georgia Press, 1966.

Hornstein, L. H. "Analysis of Imagery: A Critique of Literary Method." *Publication of the Modern Language Association*, LVII (1942), 638–53.

Howe, Irving. "On Flannery O'Connor." *New York Review of Books*, September 30, 1965, 16.

Hunt, J. W. *William Faulkner: Art in Theological Tension*. Syracuse: Syracuse University Press, 1965.

James, Henry. *Hawthorne*. Ithaca: Cornell University Press, 1956.

Jones, B. C. "Depth Psychology and Literary Study." *Midcontinent American Studies Journal*, V (1964), 50–56.

Joselyn, Sister M. "Thematic Centers in 'The Displaced Person.'" *Studies in Short Fiction*, I (Winter, 1964), 85–92.

Kayser, Wolfgang. *The Grotesque in Art and Literature*. Translated by Ulrich Weisstein. New York: McGraw-Hill, 1966.

Kellogg, G. *The Vital Tradition*. Chicago: Loyola University Press, 1970.

Kolb, H. *The Illusion of Life: American Realism as a Literary Form*. Charlottesville: University Press of Virginia, 1969.

Krieger, Murray. "Mediation, Language, and Vision in the Reading of Literature." In *Interpretation: Theory and Practice*, edited by C. S. Singleton. Baltimore: Johns Hopkins University Press, 1969.

Kroeber, Karl. *Styles in Fictional Structure*. Princeton: Princeton University Press, 1971.

Lorch, Thomas M. "Flannery O'Connor: Christian Allegorist." *Critique*, X (1968), 75–76.

Malin, Irving. *New American Gothic*. Carbondale: Southern Illinois University Press, 1962.

———. "Flannery O'Connor and the Grotesque." In *The Added Dimension: The Art and Mind of Flannery O'Connor*, edited by M. J. Friedman and L. A. Lawson. New York: Fordham University Press, 1966.

Martin, Carter W. *The True Country: Themes in the Fiction of Flannery O'Connor*. Nashville: Vanderbilt University Press, 1968.

Matthiessen, F. O. *American Renaissance: Art and Expression in the Age of Emerson and Whitman*. New York: Oxford University Press, 1968.

McCarthy, Mary. "Settling the Colonel's Hash." In *A Grammar of Literary Criticism*, edited by L. S. Hall. New York: Macmillan, 1965, 340–48.

Milder, R. "The Protestantism of Flannery O'Connor." *Southern Review*, XI (October, 1975), 802–19.

Minter, D. *The Interpreted Design as a Structural Principle in American Prose*. New Haven: Yale University Press, 1969.

Montgomery, M. "The Sense of Violation: Notes Toward a Definition of Southern Fiction." *Georgia Review*, IX (Fall, 1965), 278–87.

Mooney, Harry J., Jr. "Moments of Eternity: A Study in the Short Stories of Flannery O'Connor." In *The Shapeless God*, edited by Harry J. Mooney, Jr., and Thomas F. Staley. Pittsburgh: University of Pittsburgh Press, 1968.

Mueller, William R. *The Prophetic Voice in Modern Fiction*. Garden City: Doubleday, Anchor, 1966.

Muller, Gilbert H. *Nightmares and Visions*. Athens: University of Georgia Press, 1972.

———. "The City of Woe: Flannery O'Connor's Dantean Vision." *Georgia Review*, XXIII (Summer, 1969), 206–13.

Mullins, C. Ross, Jr. "Flannery O'Connor: An Interview." *Jubilee*, XI (June, 1963), 32–35.

O'Connor, Flannery. *The Complete Stories of Flannery O'Connor*. Edited by Sally Fitzgerald. New York: Farrar, Straus, Giroux, 1971.

———. *Everything That Rises Must Converge*. New York: Farrar, Straus, Giroux, 1965.

———. *A Good Man Is Hard to Find and Other Stories*. New York: Harcourt, Brace, 1955.

———. *The Habit of Being: Letters of Flannery O'Connor*. Edited by Sally Fitzgerald. New York: Farrar, Straus, Giroux, 1979.

———. *Mystery and Manners: Occasional Prose*. Edited by Sally and Robert Fitzgerald. New York: Farrar, Straus, Giroux, 1970.

———. *The Violent Bear It Away*. New York: Farrar, Straus, Giroux, 1960.

———. *Wise Blood*. 2nd ed. With an Introduction by the author. New York: Farrar, Straus, Giroux, 1962.

Ortega y Gasset, José. *The Dehumanization of Art and Other Writings on Art and Culture*. Translated by W. R. Trask. Garden City: Doubleday, 1956.

Orvell, Miles. *Invisible Parade: The Fiction of Flannery O'Connor*. Philadelphia: Temple University Press, 1972.

Richards, I. A. *The Philosophy of Rhetoric*. New York: Oxford University Press, 1936.

Ruskin, John. *The Complete Works of John Ruskin*. Vol. XI. Edited by G. T. Cook and A. Wedderburn. London: George Allen, 1904.

San Juan, Epifanio, Jr. *James Joyce and the Craft of Fiction*. Rutherford: Fairleigh Dickinson University Press, 1972.

Scott, Nathan A., Jr. *The Broken Center: Studies in the Theological Horizon of Modern Literature*. New Haven: Yale University Press, 1966.

Sebeok, T. A., ed. *Style in Language*. Cambridge: Massachusetts Institute of Technology Press, 1960.

Sherry, G. E. "An Interview with Flannery O'Connor." *Critic*, XXI (June–July, 1963), 29–31.

Singleton, C. S., ed. *Interpretation: Theory and Practice*. Baltimore: Johns Hopkins University Press, 1969.

Snell, Bruno. *The Discovery of Mind*. Cambridge: Harvard University Press, 1953.

Stephens, Martha. *The Question of Flannery O'Connor*. Baton Rouge: Louisiana State University Press, 1973.

Stern, Richard. "Flannery O'Connor: A Remembrance and Some Letters." *Shenandoah*, XVI (Winter, 1965), 22–41.

Stratford, Philip. *Faith and Fiction: Creative Process in Greene and Mauriac*. Notre Dame: University of Notre Dame Press, 1964.

Sullivan, Walter. *Death by Melancholy: Essays on Modern Southern Fiction*. Baton Rouge: Louisiana State University Press, 1972.

———. "The Continuing Renascence: Southern Fiction in the 50s." In *South: Modern Southern Literature in Its Cultural Setting*, edited by L. D. Rubin and R. D. Jacobs. New York: Doubleday, 1961.

Tate, J. O. "Faith and Fiction: Flannery O'Connor and the Problem of Belief." *Flannery O'Connor Bulletin*, V (1976), 105–11.

Thompson, E. "The Russian Formalists and the New Critics: Two Types of the Close Reading of the Text." *Southern Humanities Review*, IV (1970), 145–54.

Trowbridge, Clinton W. "The Symbolic Vision of Flannery O'Connor: Patterns of Imagery in *The Violent Bear It Away*." *Sewanee Review*, LXXVI (Spring, 1968), 298–318.

Van Buren, P. M. *The Edges of Language: An Essay in the Logic of a Religion*. New York: Macmillan, 1972.

Watts, Alan W. *Myth and Ritual in Christianity*. Boston: Beacon Press, 1968.

Wellek, René, and Austin Warren. *Theory of Literature*. New York: Harcourt, Brace and World, 1956.

Whalley, George. "From Symbol and Myth." In *A Grammar of Literary Criticism*, edited by L. S. Hall. New York: Macmillan, 1965, 349–52.

————. "A Note on Allegory." In *A Grammar of Literary Criticism*, edited by L. S. Hall. New York: Macmillan, 1965, 353–55.

Wheelwright, Philip. *Metaphor and Reality*. Bloomington: Indiana University Press, 1962.

Wimsatt, W. K. "Verbal Style, Logical and Counterlogical." *Publication of the Modern Language Association*, LXV (1950), 5–20.

————. *The Verbal Icon*. New York: Farrar, Straus and Cudahy, 1954.

Wittgenstein, Ludwig. *Philosophical Investigations*. Translated by G. E. M. Anscombe. Oxford: Basil Blackwell, 1967.

Index